Promises of the Word

Ron Stieglitz

Your testimonies are my heritage forever,
for they are the joy of my heart.

—Psalm 119:111

ISBN 979-8-89130-719-3 (paperback)
ISBN 979-8-89130-720-9 (digital)

Christian Faith Publishing
832 Park Avenue
Meadville, PA 16335
www.christianfaithpublishing.com

Printed in the United States of America

To Gina, Amy, Tari, and Ryan—my dear children—you each have been baptized in the name of the Father, the Son, and the Holy Spirit and made your promise at your confirmation. You are each my favorite child. Your mom and I will love you eternally.

Acknowledgments

Rev. Nathan Lewis, pastor Christ of the Bay Lutheran Church, and Chris Nelson, executive director of Northeastern Wisconsin Lutheran High School, read the text and suggested changes that clarified it as well as my thoughts. I thank them and appreciate their comments. However, any errors are solely mine. My wife, Bev, not only read the text and helped with the detailed proofing but also provided love and support without which I could not have completed this project.

Introduction

For the Lord is good; his steadfast love endures forever,
and his faithfulness to all generations.
—Psalm 100:5

I am certain that little can be written about God's promises that is truly new. As Ecclesiastes 1:9 points out, "There is nothing new under the sun." Yet there are still things that can be said about them. They can be looked at more closely, understood more clearly, and related and applied to our lives more directly. Some of us never have thought deeply about them or appreciated them fully. We recognize some of the big ones; God promises us eternal life, but that's in the future. Although our hope in that is sure, we first have to live out our lives to experience that blessing. Our life journey is filled with many bumps and obstacles along the way. He also promises to be with us through our journey and to provide a helper, the Holy Spirit, to help us make the trip. Let us not overlook or discount those promises. If we are not aware of and do not know those promises, we do not fully know God and his Savior son Jesus.

Promises! Promises?

It is easy to make promises—it is hard work to keep them.
—Boris Johnson

Have you ever made a promise? Have you ever broken a promise? Of course, you have. We all have. We humans are great promise makers. We are not quite as good as promise keepers. A little more than seven hundred years before the birth of Jesus, the prophet Hosea lamented the same problem with his culture.

They utter mere words; with empty oaths
they make covenants; so judgment springs up
like poisonous weeds in the furrows of the field.
(Hosea 10:4)

The prophet who worked in the northern kingdom of Israel shortly before its fall to the Assyrians was deeply concerned with the conditions he found in the culture and courts of his country. It seems that things have not changed. Let's take a look at some easy targets first. There are many. Some might make us knowingly say, "Right on," whereas others might make us a little uncomfortable. Some of them might cause us pause to think about what we promise ourselves and others.

Promises Made, Promises Broken

In this day and age of acrimony and bitter divisions, politicians immediately come to mind. Politicians are perhaps the most prolific makers of promises. Their promises come fast and furious as election cycles heat up. Most are forgotten, excused, or revised after an election. Assurances are made of an open and transparent administration, cooperation with those across the aisle, and fiscal responsibility with lower deficits. There will be more jobs with higher wages, better roads, better schools with free tuition, and social programs that will end poverty, all with lower taxes. How can we not respond positively; there is something for everyone. But what is the record on these and others? How many are fulfilled or even seriously addressed?

Financial advisors and brokers promise stock market growth, high return rates, increasing real estate values, and investment opportunities with quick profits that we can't miss. They also promise to manage our money honestly and for our best interests. However, when the stock market plunges, a recession hits, or the hot tip turns out to be a Ponzi scheme, large amounts of money, even life savings, might be lost. And that cheerful broker has realized more gains from our accounts than we did and might have even embezzled from them.

College athletes promise allegiance to the team and the college or university only to enter the transfer portal after one year to look for a better opportunity. Professional athletes love the city and their teammates. They promise their fans all-out effort all the time, fantastic games, and sure championships. Then games are lost, championships do not materialize, and another team offers more money.

We may grumble about all those broken promises and how we do not understand that type of behavior. However, when we look closer at home, we find behavior that makes us uncomfortable when we think about it. As parents, we promise to take our children to someplace special on Saturday but are too tired to do so. We promise to attend their important game or performance but work intervenes. How about New Year's resolutions? We promise, if only to ourselves to lose weight, exercise more, eat more healthy food, and forgo that second cocktail after dinner each night. We might also promise to be a better spouse and a more understanding neighbor, to be kinder to customer service agents, and to attend church more regularly. What's our batting average on those? Too often we do not fulfill those promises and rationalize our behavior in not doing so.

Promises Made, Promises Kept

In contrast to the promises that we make and often break, God's promises are solid and sure. God's Word is rich with promises. They are promises that touch every aspect of our lives, promises that when we recognize and appreciate them provide meaning and comfort. They are found sprinkled throughout the Scriptures more densely than we might have realized.

In the Old Testament, promises were transmitted to and through individuals and prophets who clearly indicate that they come from God. In the New Testament, we hear them in the very words of Jesus. Thankfully, they are not founded on us. Perhaps that is the best news of all. God's promises do not depend on what they are, how important they seem to be to us and our resolve, or how hard we try to live up to them. Many passages in the Word speak of God's promises to his Old-Testament-chosen people and individuals and to New Testament Christians. Some of those promises are crystal clear. Some are less than clear and require unpacking while others are of the *read-over* variety that we often go past unless we are paying close attention. History shows us that all those promises are kept. Some are quite specific and may pertain only to a single battle or the circumstances of a particular individual. Others are applicable to believers anywhere at any time. Some of these covenants contained both short-term answers to prayers but with pledges of future blessings. God's Word is the most important word that we will ever hear or read and in that Word are the most important promises that will ever be made to us.

God made some fantastic promises in the Bible, some of which many of us are at least somewhat familiar. In the Old Testament, the Israelites had been on the road for forty years on their long and circuitous trek to the promised land following their escape from bondage in Egypt. When they finally crossed the Jordan River, they ran into resistance from the people living in the area. God then promised Joshua, the Hebrew general, victory in his battle for the city of Jericho.

> And the Lord said to Joshua, "See, I have
> given Jericho into your hand, with its king and
> mighty men of valor." (Joshua 6:2)

He then outlined an unusual plan of attack. Simply march around the walls of Jericho for six days. Then on the seventh day have the priests blow horns and the people shout, and as the song goes; the walls came tumbling down. The lesson: Believe and just do it!

In the New Testament Jesus, God's Son, even extended promises to foreigners who were despised by most Jews. When Jesus entered the city of Capernaum, he was approached by a centurion, a Roman soldier, and an officer, who appealed to him on behalf of one of his servants.

> And he [Jesus] said to him, "I will come and
> heal him." But the centurion replied, "Lord, I am
> not worthy to have you come under my roof,
> but only say the word, and my servant will be
> healed." (Matthew 8:7–8)

The officer deferred, saying that he was not important enough for Jesus to come to his house, but he believed that just a word from Jesus would heal his servant. Jesus commended his faith and continued,

> I tell you, many will come from east and
> west and recline at the table with Abraham, Isaac,
> and Jacob in the kingdom of heaven. (Matthew
> 8:11)

This is one of the *read-over* promises indicating that the Gentiles will have a place in heaven.

> And to the centurion Jesus said, "Go; let
> it be done for you as you have believed." And

the servant was healed at that very moment.
(Matthew 8:13)

The lesson: Believe and ask!

The promises to Joshua and the Roman centurion were seemingly made directly to individuals, but both had much wider and more significant implications. One gave the Israelites confidence to continue to take possession of the promised land. The other gave healing to a servant of a Gentile and assurance that non-Jews are included in God's kingdom. By the way, this was not the first time that Gentiles were promised a place in God's kingdom.

In both the Old Testament and the New Testament, God delivered his promises, commandments, and other messages in a number of ways. They came in dreams, visions, by angelic messengers, and apparently in some cases directly by face-to-face encounters (Appendix 1). Let's consider some of those promises and learn the everlasting value and comfort that they have for us.

Questions for Thought and Discussion

1. How do you think the healing of the centurion's servant would have been received by the Jews in the context of their first-century culture? Why might it have been controversial, especially for the Pharisees?
2. Why is it so difficult for us to keep our promises?
3. In your estimation, do people promise more and deliver less now than in the past? Why or why not?

Old Testament Promises

Not one word of all the good promises that the LORD had made
to the house of Israel had failed; all came to pass.

—Joshua 21:45

God's promises are found throughout the Old Testament Scriptures. Some of them promise temporal blessings such as long life or children, whereas others promise amazing long-term blessings. Some are quite direct with short-term outcomes clearly defined whereas others are rather complex and contain temporal and long-term and even eternal messianic prophecies. Again, we should note, as in the previous section, some were directed toward a specific individual, but others were made with groups of people most often with God's chosen people the Israelite nation.

Promises of Temporal Blessings

And I will put my Spirit within you, and you shall
live, and I will place you in your own land.
—Ezekiel 37:14

In Old Testament times, God initiated a number of covenants or agreements with the patriarchs, individuals, and the Israelite nation (Appendix 2). A biblical covenant refers to a permanent all-encompassing agreement between God and men. God was always the initiator, not humans. God proposed the requirements, and set the expectations. Unfortunately, because fallible humans were involved, they usually were unable or unwilling to fulfill the conditions of the agreements.

God Promises a Child

The patriarch Abraham, whose name God changed from Abram, is considered the father of the Hebrew nation. God had promised him several times that he would be the forerunner of many nations. However, as he approached old age, he and his wife were still childless. In the prevailing culture of Abraham's time, childless women were often pitied, not respected, and also in danger of being destitute in their old age. Men greatly valued children as heirs and to continue the family line. Human reasoning came into play, and he began to question how God's promise was to be fulfilled. Apparently, his wife, Sarai, suggested that he father heirs by her maidservant, Hagar.

Taking matters into his own hands, he fathered a son by Hagar when he was eighty-six. As you might expect, even though his wife, Sarai, had given him permission, things did not go well. After she conceived, Hagar behaved contemptuously toward Sarai, and there was friction between the two women. Abraham loved the boy he named Ishmael and first thought that he would be the promised heir, but God had other plans.

Sarai prodded Abraham to send Hagar and Ishmael away, and even though he was very reluctant to do so, following God's directions, he did after God promised to take care of the two. Abraham had given her some provisions and water, but when they were gone, Hagar was despondent and prepared to let the boy die. God said to Hagar,

> Up! Lift up the boy, and hold him fast
> with your hand, for I will make him into a great
> nation. (Genesis 21:18)

God provided a water well, and they were saved. Ishmael became the progenitor of the Ishmaelite nation mentioned a number of times in the Old Testament that traced its lineage from Abraham through Ishmael. One of the many nations promised to him.

Twelve or thirteen years later, God changed Sarai's name to Sarah and again promised Abraham a son by her. Despite this renewed promise, Abraham was still having difficulty accepting it as reality. In fact, he was incredulous when God again promised him an heir.

> Then Abraham fell on his face and laughed
> and said to himself, "Shall a child be born to a
> man who is a hundred years old? Shall Sarah,
> who is ninety years old, bear a child?" (Genesis
> 17:17)

God also told Abraham that he would return to him about the same time the following year and that Sarah would bear him a son. But a promise from God is a promise fulfilled.

> And Sarah conceived and bore Abraham a
> son in his old age at the time which God had
> spoken to him. Abraham called the name of his
> son who was born to him, whom Sarah bore him,
> Isaac. (Genesis 21:2–3)

This was the fulfillment of a promise made to a childless couple in their old age. The child Isaac was the second of the three great patriarchs of the Israelites. The lesson here: The Lord does not need our help to fulfill his promises!

God Promises a Homeland

The promise of a rich land for the Israelites and that they would grow into a great nation resounds throughout the early books of the Old Testament. God reiterated that pledge over many years to rather small groups of people to encourage them to look forward to the time when they would live in their own land. The pledge goes far beyond any individual or family. This important promise was restated to each of the three patriarchs in turn and reached its culmination with the Exodus of the Israelites from Egypt led by Moses. Later, it is restated or alluded to in a number of other Old Testament passages as a reminder for the people to be thankful for this gift and to encourage them to follow the Lord's commands. That is especially the case in the book of Joshua in which the portions of Canaan allotted to each tribe are referred to as their inheritance. This term makes it clear that the land is a gift from God and not the result of any effort or merit by the Israelites.

The promise of a homeland was first made to Abraham, called Abram at the time. Abram lived in Ur which was a city along the Euphrates River somewhat north of the Persian Gulf. Abram and his family left Ur and traveled northwestward to the city of Haran in Mesopotamia, and although Canaan was their ultimate destination, they settled in the area for some time. It was there that the Lord called him to leave his country and his family and go to a land God would show him.

> Now the LORD said to Abram, "Go from
> your country and your kindred and your father's
> house to the land that I will show you." (Genesis
> 12:1)

Although he and his wife were both along in years, he was seventy-five at the time, he went. With his family and flocks, he traveled slowly to the south until he reached Canaan and even went as far as Egypt. The lesson here: Have faith and go when we are called!

More than seventy years later, God answered the prayer of Abraham's son, Isaac, when his wife Rebekah gave birth to twin boys. The older boy was named Esau. The other was Jacob destined to be the third of the great patriarchs. Esau grew into a hunter and outdoorsman. Jacob was a quiet thoughtful man and perhaps a little deceitful. Despite the family problems, God visited Isaac and renewed his promise of land.

> Sojourn in this land, and I will be with you
> and will bless you, for to you and to your off
> spring I will give all these lands, and I will estab
> lish the oath that I swore to Abraham your father.
> (Genesis 26:3)

God did bless Isaac, and he became prosperous with flocks of sheep and herds of cattle as well as other gifts. However, because of an impetuous decision and lack of attention, Esau was maneuvered by Jacob into selling his birthright as the oldest son and losing the accompanying blessing by Isaac. As you might expect, this did nothing to foster brotherly love between Esau and Jacob. The sharp sibling rivalry between the two boys was not resolved for many years.

To secure a suitable wife for his son Jacob and to protect him from Esau's anger, Isaac at his wife's encouragement sent Jacob on a trip to his uncle Laban in a place known as Paddan Aram. This was an area around the city of Ur in southern Mesopotamia where Abraham had originally lived before beginning his move to Canaan. On the way, Jacob stopped for a night of rest and made himself comfortable by using a rock for a pillow. Not a choice we are likely to make although some motel pillows I have used might qualify. He had an unusual dream about a ladder to heaven with angels going up and down. In the dream, God again restated the promise of land.

> And behold, the LORD stood above it and
> said, "I am the LORD, the God of Abraham your
> father and the God of Isaac. The land on which
> you lie I will give to you and to your offspring."
> (Genesis 28:13)

Some commentators have held that this strange dream was given to assure Jacob that despite deceitful dealings with his family, God was there to receive his requests and to send strength and guidance in turn.

Laban had two daughters, Leah the older and Rachel the younger whom Jacob loved. He agreed to serve his uncle for seven years for the hand of Rachel; however, when the time came for the marriage to take place, Laban substituted Leah for Rachel and required Jacob to serve another seven years for her. Perhaps, there is a bit of deceitful turnabout here. The details of the contentious and complicated relationship between Jacob and his uncle need not concern us here. Eventually, after fleeing from Laban and his sons, Jacob struck a treaty of peace with him. As they grew older, Esau forgave Jacob, and the brothers reconciled. Esau's descendants grew into the nation of Edom, another nation that traced its roots back to Abraham.

God then changed Jacob's name to Israel, directed him to return to the land of his fathers, and promised that he would bless and guide him.

> And God said to him, "I am God Almighty:
> be fruitful and multiply. A nation and a company
> of nations shall come from you, and kings shall
> come from your own body. The land that I gave
> to Abraham and Isaac I will give to you, and I
> will give the land to your offspring after you."
> (Genesis 35:11–12)

Note that God again promised that many nations would arise from the line of the patriarchs and reaffirmed the long-continued promise of a homeland. In the somewhat distant future, God would fulfill those promises in a most unusual way by rescuing enslaved but recalcitrant people and guiding them to a land of their own.

Jacob prospered over a long lifetime. Leah and Rachel and two of their slave women, Zilpah and Bilah, bore Jacob's twelve sons who are considered the founders of the Israelite tribes. The most well-known of his sons, Joseph, was sold into slavery by his brothers and carried off to Egypt. Through a series of events guided by God, he became a high-ranking official of the Egyptian Pharaoh and saved his father, brothers, and their families from famine. He arranged to settle them in a part of Egypt known as Goshen where over the next approximately four hundred years they multiplied and grew into numerous people as promised, first in freedom and later as oppressed slaves. If you are unfamiliar with Joseph's story, it is told in the last chapters of Genesis, and it is worth the time to read. It is one of the longest, if not the longest, story about an individual in the Old Testament. It has been made into an entertaining musical, *Joseph and the Amazing Technicolor Dreamcoat*, with music by Andrew Lloyd Webber. It is enjoyable and also well worth attending.

Just before their escape from Egypt known as the Exodus, God again promised the Israelites through the great prophet Moses that they would inherit a rich land with its towns and cities.

> Then the LORD said, "I have surely seen the affliction of my people who are in Egypt and have heard their cry because of their taskmasters. I know their sufferings, and I have come down to deliver them out of the hand of the Egyptians and to bring them up out of that land to a good and broad land, a land flowing with milk and honey." (Exodus 3:7–8)

Moses had fled Egypt years earlier after he killed an Egyptian slave overlord. As a fugitive, he did not exactly relish the chance to return to Egypt when he was called by God to lead the Israelites and face the powerful Pharaoh. As we so often do when asked to undertake a difficult and possibly time-consuming church project, he took the why-me approach and offered a number of excuses.

We have the best excuses stored up for such times. I have developed a great collection of excuses. Perhaps you would like to borrow one of them?

- "Sorry, Pastor, I am so busy at work. I do not have the time to work on the outreach project just now."
- "Karen, I know you need help with this project, but I have a young family, and they take up so much of my time."
- "Pastor, I have thought it over, and I'm just not qualified to be the chairman of that committee."
- "Mike, I know I should get involved with that project, but I have been so tired lately. I'm not sure that I would do a good job."
- "What evening does that committee meet, Pastor? Oh, that's too bad."
- This is a fill-in-the-blank one: "[I, my daughter, my son, my wife] has [a softball game, dance lessons, band practice, club meeting] at the same time."
- "You know, Pastor, Joan is the chair of that committee, and our ideas just don't match."
- "I've done my share, and it's time for someone else to step up." (This might be my favorite.)

It took a while for Moses to be convinced that he was the man for the job. He was not at all certain that he was up to the task or that the Israelites would listen to him. Eventually, God overcame Moses's objections and insecurities and provided him with assistants and signs to accomplish the task of freeing his people. To reassure him and strengthen his resolve, God again promised,

"I will bring you into the land that I swore
to give to Abraham, to Isaac, and to Jacob. I will

give it to you for possession. I am the LORD."
(Exodus 6:8)

Moses knew that it would be a dangerous and difficult assignment that would try his patience. He just didn't know how frustrating and trying it would be.

During their journey, God initiated a covenant with the Israelites at Mount Sinai that they first promised to obey, then broke, and finally reaffirmed. Moses led the people to the east side of the Jordan River but was forbidden by God to enter the promised land. Joshua, the army general, and Moses's longtime assistant assumed the leadership role and led the Israelites across the Jordan River. Through a series of military campaigns, the people living in Canaan were mostly conquered, and their lands were divided among the tribes as their inheritance.

> Thus the LORD gave to Israel all the land
> that he swore to give to their fathers. And they
> took possession of it and they settled there.
> (Joshua 21:43)

It is interesting to note that when the land was allotted to the tribes, the tribe of Levi did not receive a specific area. Instead, the tribe received cities scattered throughout the nation based on a promise made by Moses because of their service in helping to end the episode of the golden calf (Appendix 3). God had fulfilled his promise, and now it was up to the Israelites to live up to the terms of the covenant. It was a requirement that they often found difficult to accomplish.

God Promises Additional Blessings

Beyond promising freedom from the Egyptians and that the Israelites would take possession of a new land, God also promised more specific temporal blessings. In those Old Testament covenants, there was often an *if/then* requirement that the human participants had to fulfill. When Moses was leading the people, God established through his laws and regulations that governed all aspects of Hebrew society. One such regulation was the sabbatical year. Every seven years, all creditors were to be released from the debts that they owed to other members of the nation. The Lord then promised blessings but with a caveat.

> But there will be no poor among you; for the LORD will bless you in the land that the LORD your God is giving you for an inheritance to possess—if only you will strictly obey the voice of the LORD your God, being careful to do all this commandment that I command you today. For the LORD your God will bless you as he promised you, you shall lend to many nations, but you shall not borrow, and you shall rule over many nations, but they shall not rule over you. (Deuteronomy 15:4–6)

This is an example of a promise with an *if/then* clause; obey the voice of the Lord and the promise will be fulfilled. The LORD had promised them the land. Now he promised them blessings and that the relatively small group of Hebrews would become a wealthy and influential nation. All they had to do was to obey all his commands. Here again is that troublesome *if/then* requirement. The lesson here: It is not always easy to keep a promise, especially one made to the Lord.

God elaborated on his promise of blessings several times and in several ways. He wanted his people to make him first in their lives and to honor him so that he could in return provide blessings for them.

> Honor the LORD with your wealth and with the first fruits of all your produce; then your barns will be filled with plenty, and your vats will be bursting with wine. (Proverbs 3:9–10)

He also wanted them to be generous and loving to others rather than hoard wealth for their own use.

> Whoever brings blessings will be enriched,
> and one who waters will himself will be watered.
> (Proverbs 11:25)

These are good and useful things for us New Testament Christians to think about and apply to our lives as well. God wants us to make him first in our lives and honor him and be kind and compassionate to other people. The lesson here: Honor the Lord and be generous and blessings will follow.

There is a caution here. These verses should not be used to support the popular idea of a prosperity gospel. The verses in Proverbs 3 say that the barns will be filled and that the vats will be bursting with wine. They do not say to build more barns and more vats so that God will fill them with unending riches. Proverbs 11 promises blessings, but blessings go far beyond monetary value. Personal good health, a healthy and happy family, a strong marriage, a satisfying occupation, and life in a free nation that recognizes religious freedom are all invaluable blessings. To think that if we believe deeply enough, pray hard enough, and do enough good, we will be rewarded with riches seems to be not only a misunderstanding of God's promises but also a perversion of their meaning. As we shall see, God also promises that we will experience things that are anything but pleasant no matter how strong our faith is.

Questions for Thought and Discussion

1. Do you feel that the temporal promises God made to the patriarchs are of any relevance and importance for Christians today?
2. Why would God change the names of Abram to Abraham, Sarai to Sarah, and Jacob to Israel?
3. God promised Abraham and the other patriarchs a land of their own many years before it actually happened. Do you

suppose that there was a practical reason for that? How did God use the people's captivity in Egypt to fulfill that promise?

4. Do you have a favorite excuse to use to slip out of difficult or time-consuming tasks? What is it?

Promises of Eternal Blessings

Let your steadfast love comfort me according
to your promise to your servant.
—Psalm 119:76

In the Old Testament covenants with the patriarchs and later the Israelite nation, God made many promises that also carried long term, that is, eternal blessings to the believers of that time and also to those of New Testament time. Let's look more closely at some of those Old Testament covenants we have already considered to learn some additional things from them.

God's Promises to the Patriarchs

In the original covenant with Abram instructing him to leave his homeland, God also included a somewhat unclear article that promised he would have an important future impact. God said,

> And I will make of you a great nation, and I will bless you and make your name great, so that you will be a blessing. I will bless those who bless you, and him who dishonors you I will curse, and in you all the families of the earth shall be blessed. (Genesis 12:2–3)

This leads to the question, "How is it possible that all families of the earth will be blessed through a humble nomad who lived and wandered the Middle Eastern desert thousands of years ago?" Although God promised that a great nation would come from Abram, was this to mean that his influence would spread throughout the world of his time, or did it imply something more? Later, God added to his covenant when he renamed Abram Abraham:

> Behold, my covenant is with you, and you shall be the father of a multitude of nations. No longer shall your name be called Abram, but your name shall be Abraham, for I have made you the father of a multitude of nations. (Genesis 17:4–5)

Here, God calls Abraham the father of a multitude of nations indicating a paternal relationship and that his influence will play out over time in the future. We have already learned that the descendants of both Ishmael and Esau grew into nations in their own right. That's pretty heavy stuff! Not only did he receive a message from God, but he was also told that he was to have an important legacy. A lesser man might have let that information go to his head and become proud and haughty. But Abraham was a man of faith.

Similarly, besides promising a homeland to Isaac, God added,

> I will multiply your offspring as the stars of heaven and will give to your offspring all these lands. And in your offspring all the nations of the earth shall be blessed, because Abraham obeyed my voice and kept my charge, my commandments, my statutes, and my laws. (Genesis 26:4–5)

This more clearly states that all nations will be blessed through Isaac's descendants again implying a future aspect to the promise.

Despite Jacob's deceptive dealings with his father and his brother, the Lord also promised him great influence and impact through his descendants.

> "Your offspring shall be like the dust of the earth, and you shall spread abroad to the west

and to the east and to the north and to the south,
and in you and your offspring shall all the families of the earth be blessed." (Genesis 28:14)

Why should these covenants be considered as eternal? Are they not merely promises to individuals or families which suggest that there will be many descendants of considerable influence? It is true that they promised descendants but that they also promised blessings which would continue through time and benefit all the nations of the earth. With the words "all families of the earth be blessed," they also hint at something that is more clearly expressed elsewhere. That is, the kingdom of God is not a private possession of the Jews and that a more inclusive covenant was to come.

God's Promises to the Hebrew People

God chose the Hebrews and consecrated them, that is, set them apart for a special purpose—the unique mission of carrying out his plan of salvation.

For you are a people holy to the LORD your
God. The LORD your God has chosen you to be
a people for his treasured possession, out of all
the peoples who were on the face of the earth.
(Deuteronomy 7:6)

The mission was to protect but not hoard God's plan of salvation only for Jews. Eventually they were to carry it to all nations and to serve as a witness to God's grace. Many years after the patriarchs, the great prophet Isaiah who worked in the southern kingdom of Judah sometime before 700 BC clearly saw that mission.

The LORD has bared his holy arm before the
eyes of all nations, and all the ends of the earth
shall see the salvation of our God. (Isaiah 52:10)

This passage directly states what had been hinted at in the covenants with the patriarchs; the promise that the Gentiles also are to receive salvation and are to be included in God's kingdom. It is of extreme importance to Christians today because most Christians are Gentiles. This is a marvelous promise made to us by God through a prophet almost three thousand years ago.

The Jews of Jesus's day seem to have believed that they were somehow saved simply because they descended from Abraham, and by keeping the Law, they could earn salvation. They thought that Abraham was rewarded for what he did rather than for his faith in God. The apostle Paul cleared up that confusion and false notion.

> Know then that it is those of faith who are the sons of Abraham. And the Scripture, foreseeing that God would justify the Gentiles by faith, preach the gospel beforehand to Abraham, saying, "In you shall all the nations be blessed." So then, those who are of faith are blessed along with Abraham, the man of faith. (Galatians 3:7–9)

This passage explains Abraham's contribution and clarifies those Old Testament passages that promise blessings to all the nations of the earth. The lesson here: We are saved by faith and not by works or by keeping the law.

Questions for Thought and Discussion

1. Do you think that Abraham and his contemporaries fully understood the covenants that God made with him? Why or why not?
2. How did the pride of being descendants of Abraham result in the Jews miss interpreting the significance of Abraham?
3. In what ways did the Jews carry out their selection as special people selected by God? In what ways did they fail?

Promises of the Messiah

I know that Messiah is coming.

—John 4:25

Something even more remarkable was included in those Old Testament promises to the patriarchs and the Israelite nation besides a homeland and the formation of many nations. It was a widely held belief among the Old Testament Jewish people that a Messiah, the *anointed* one, known by the Greek word Christ in the New Testament, would appear to lead the nation and to return it to a place of honor and power in the world. To be anointed signifies that a person was selected and set apart and belonged to God for a special purpose. Following the reign of King Solomon, the united nation was divided into two separate kingdoms, Israel in the north and Judah to the south. As might be expected, their influence, power, and wealth declined and never again approached that of the United Kingdom under Solomon. Eventually both were conquered and sent into exile. First, Israel was destroyed by the Assyrians about 720 BC, and little more than a century or so later, Judah was overrun by the Babylonians. Because of this, there was great longing and hope for a heroic leader who would reestablish Israel as a strong and glorious nation.

The concept of a Messiah was somewhat ill-defined as he had been prophesied in a number of veiled references. His characteristics and purpose were perhaps misunderstood. The Jews who returned from exile and those who continued to live in what we now call the Holy Land were especially hopeful of a Messiah who would come to deliver them from the domination of foreign powers and especially from Rome. Most believed and hoped that he would be a heroic figure who would establish a glorious earthly kingdom. Perhaps this mistaken concept rather than that of a suffering servant as portrayed by the prophets contributed to the reluctance of many Jews to accept Jesus as the Christ.

God's First Promise of a Messiah

Long before the patriarchs, in fact in the Garden of Eden shortly after the fall, God directed a curse toward Satan and promised a savior to come.

> The LORD God said to the serpent, "Because you have done this, cursed are you above all livestock and above all beasts of the field; on your belly you shall go, and dust you shall eat all the days of your life. I will put enmity between you and the woman, and between your offspring and her offspring, he shall bruise your head, and you shall bruise his heel." (Genesis 3:14–15)

The curse is clear, the promise less so. This might be one of the *read-over* promises for many of us. Enmity is the condition of hatred and hostility between individuals, groups, or nations. It might be understood as the state of continual warfare among different groups. It could also be taken quite literally as the fear and revulsion that most humans have for snakes. However, it is best interpreted as that one of Eve's offspring would wage spiritual warfare with and eventually overcome the sons of Satan. The *New International Version* reads "crush your head" which might be somewhat more specific than that of the *English Standard Version* "bruise your head" in the passage above. It is the first promise of the Messiah.

God's Messianic Promises to the Patriarchs

When studied more closely, several of the covenants that God initiated with the Israelites also contain the promise of a special offspring of the patriarchs. Perhaps the most specific promise of a very special descendent was given to Abraham shortly after he was tested by God to sacrifice his son Isaac. By faith, he was able to pass the test. As a father, I can imagine his anguish and relate to his great relief when Isaac was spared. The promise was announced to Abraham by the angel of the Lord who is usually taken to be the preincarnate Jesus.

> I will surely bless you, and I will surely multiply your offspring as the stars of heaven and as the sand that is on the seashore. And your offspring shall possess the gate of his enemies, and in your offspring shall all nations of the earth be blessed, because you have obeyed my voice. (Genesis 22:17–18)

Scholars who study the ancient Hebrew texts and the later Greek translations tell us that the construction and word choices reveal a dichotomy in this promise which is of the utmost importance. The first part of the promise addresses Abraham's descendants (plural) who will greatly increase in number and establish the other promised nations. The second part addresses a specific descendent (singular) through whom all nations will be blessed. Clearly this is a reference to the Messiah. In the New Testament, the apostle Paul recognized the same truth in that promise and pointed to its fulfillment in the man Jesus.

> Now the promises were made to Abraham and to his offspring. It does not say, "And to offsprings," referring to many, but referring to one, "And to your offspring, who is Christ." (Galatians 3:16)

God said similar things to Isaac and Jacob in the extensions of the Genesis passages quoted earlier. In the New Testament, the author of the book of Hebrews writes about the patriarchs and their families making an important point.

> These all died in faith, not having received the things promised, but having seen them and greeted them from afar, and having acknowledged that they were strangers and exiles on the earth. (Hebrews 11:13)

From the human side, faith is the critical element of the promise. It is possible that Eve, the patriarchs, and even David thought and hoped that their child was the promised Messiah. But that was not the case. None of them had the privilege of seeing the Messiah with their own eyes, but they were allowed a glimpse of the future. Despite being weak humans, each one believed, had faith, and carried on the promise. Although they each experienced slipups and hiccups along the way, each one moved forward and obeyed God as imperfect humans.

The pledge of a special descendent had been given, but the *how*, *when*, and *where* of his appearance was uncertain and not specified. What would he be like—a conquering hero or something else?

God's Promises to King David and His Family Line

As the centuries passed, the Jews vacillated between following the Lord or accepting the heathen gods worshiped by the nations surrounding them. At times, they even attempted to follow both and were enticed to add a heathen god or two to ensure abundant harvests and fruitful animals. Better to cover all your bases and to be safe rather than sorry. Holding to the covenant and following its demands was not so easy.

When King David ruled Israel, he hoped and prayed that he would be able to build a temple as a house for God, but that was not to be. David was a warrior, and his story is filled with examples of both great faith and obedience as well as shame and failure. For example, with faith, he opposed Goliath and honorably served Israel's first king, Saul. However, when Saul's jealousy forced him to flee, he became a hunted man and for a short time served one of the kings of Israel's archenemies, the Philistines. After becoming Israel's second king, he won great victories for the nation but also stole another man's wife and arranged for her husband's murder. Despite this, God considered him "a man after his own heart" (1 Samuel 13:14) and forgave his sins as he has for each of us. That David, one of the Old Testament heroes of faith, is portrayed with all his human failings and foibles should be a comfort to us as we daily struggle with our own sinful nature.

In a Psalm written by a man named Ethan who was probably a priest or Levite, God more directly identifies the familial lineage of the Messiah and David's place in it.

> You have said, "I have made a covenant with
> my chosen one; I have sworn to David my servant:
> I will establish your offspring forever, and build up
> your throne for all generations." (Psalm 89:3–4)

This pledge to David is a marvelous example of God's grace to sinners. King David, sometimes saint and sometimes sinner, whose lineage extends backward to Abraham is now promised a descendent who will occupy a throne forever. While this is similar to the promises made to the patriarchs, it identifies a specific person and family out of the tribes of Israel to be the ancestor of the Messiah. David's family line, which sometimes hung by a thread after the Babylonian conquest and the exile of the Israelites, was to be preserved until the Messiah would appear. He was not allowed to build the temple, but he was promised something much more enduring. He was to be the ancestor, the father, of his Lord and Savior. Think carefully about that for a minute. Consider this. How would you feel and what would be your reaction if God said to you, "Be patient. One of your descendants will be the long-promised Messiah?" What a wonder!

The prophet Isaiah ministered to the southern nation of Judah a little before 700 BC, and his book contains some of the clearest and best-known promises of the Messiah.

> There shall come forth a shoot from the
> stump of Jesse, and a branch from his roots shall

bear fruit. And the Spirit of the Lord shall rest upon him, the Spirit of wisdom and understanding, the Spirit of counsel and might, the Spirit of knowledge and the fear of the Lord. (Isaiah 11:1–2)

Here the prophet distinctly places David's family in the line of descendants leading to the Messiah. Jesse was David's father. David's family or descendants were certainly reduced in importance after the fall of Judah, but God preserved it until the time was right for the Messiah to appear. Only a stump remained of the once-royal-and-important family. In the New Testament book of Romans chapter 15, the Apostle Paul quotes this and other Old Testament verses to show that the Messiah, that is Jesus, is the long-promised savior of the Gentiles as well as the Jews.

About 630 BC and seventy or eighty years after Isaiah, the prophet Jeremiah who also worked in the southern kingdom of Judah also saw that the Lord would bless David with a special descendent.

Behold, the days are coming, declares the Lord, when I will raise up for David a righteous Branch, and he shall reign as king and deal wisely, and shall execute justice and righteousness in the land. In his days Judah will be saved, and Israel will dwell securely. And this is the name by which he will be called: "The Lord is our righteousness." (Jeremiah 23:5–6)

God was true to his word preserving David's royal family line even though his descendants no longer possessed a throne after the nation of Judah was destroyed by the Babylonians about 580 BC. David's line continued through the Babylonian exile, the return of only a remnant of the Jews about eighty years later, and a long history of subjugation by other nations.

Promises of the Messiah Made and Fulfilled

By the inspiration of God, Isaiah was led by the Holy Spirit to see not only the inclusion of the Gentiles in the kingdom of God as mentioned earlier but also the glorious birth, suffering, and death of the Messiah. Isaiah's book is so rich with promises and descriptions of the Messiah that it is difficult to take it all in and wrap your mind around it. Speaking to Ahaz, one of the kings of Judah, Isaiah seemed to have become frustrated with the king's refusal to ask for a sign from God as dangers gathered. He said,

> Hear then, O house of David! Is it too little
> for you to weary men, that you weary my God also?
> Therefore the LORD himself will give you a sign.
> Behold, the virgin shall conceive and bear a son,
> and shall call his name Immanuel. (Isaiah 7:13–14)

The house of David refers to his descendants who held the royal throne of Judah until the nation was destroyed by Babylonian armies.

Seven hundred years later in the Galilean town of Nazareth, a young virgin named Mary was found to be pregnant before having sexual relations with her betrothed husband, Joseph. Perhaps today, when almost anything is acceptable, we can't understand how much of an embarrassingly big deal this was in the culture of their time. It was a huge and concerning problem! In a dream, the angel of the Lord appeared to Joseph and told him that Mary had been conceived by the Holy Spirit. In our day, the fiancé is most likely to say, "Right! In your dreams!" However, Joseph accepted the heavenly message and proceeded with the marriage. In his Gospel, Matthew relates the story, quotes the passage from Isaiah 7:14, and explains the name Immanuel.

> All this took place to fulfill what the Lord
> had spoken by the prophet: "Behold, the virgin
> shall conceive and bear a son, and they shall call
> his name Immanuel" (which means, God with
> us). (Matthew 1:22–23)

Sometime earlier, Mary had been visited by the angel Gabriel who told her that she had found favor with God and would conceive and bear a son. Although Mary believed Gabriel's message, she still asked, "How is this possible?" This is a question that has been asked ever since, by some in humble awe and others in scornful unbelief. Gabriel provided an unequivocal answer,

> For nothing will be impossible with God.
> (Luke 1:37)

We need to recall that answer and understand its significance.

Isaiah attempted to warn Judah of the coming Assyrian invasion, but no one listened or was concerned because that was years in the future. Despite his message being turned off and scorned by the leaders and most of the people, he went on to explain that despite the coming disaster, there was promise for future peace and joy. Verses 2 through 7 of chapter 9 provide remarkable and informative promises of the Messiah. This section contains one of the most beautiful and well-known descriptions of the Messiah's birth.

> For to us a child is born, to us a son is given; and the government shall be upon his shoulder, and his name shall be called Wonderful Counselor, Mighty God, Everlasting Father, Prince of Peace. (Isaiah 9:6)

This promise came to fruition and was fully sealed when the angels announced the birth of Jesus to the shepherds in the fields near Bethlehem.

> For unto you is born this day in the city of David a Savior, who is Christ the Lord. (Luke 2:11)

Verses 2 through 7 of chapter 9 from the Old Testament book of Isaiah followed by verses 8 through 20 of chapter 2 from the New Testament book of Luke are wonderful passages for you or your children to read to the family on Christmas Eve. They are a clear, direct, and perfect complement of promise and fulfillment.

The prophet Micah, a contemporary of Isaiah, was also inspired to make a stunningly accurate prediction of the Messiah's birthplace.

> But you, O Bethlehem Ephrathah, who are too little to be among the clans of Judah, from you shall come forth for me one who is to be ruler in Israel, whose coming forth is from of old, from ancient days. (Micah 5:2)

Ephrathah was an ancient name for the town of Bethlehem. This was a well-known prophecy. When the wise men of the east arrived in Jerusalem searching for the newly born king of the Jews, they inquired about his place of birth. King Herod, apparently not well acquainted with the Scriptures himself, called together the scribes and the chief priest to learn where the Messiah was to be born. "They told him, 'In Bethlehem of Judea, for so it is written by the prophet'" (Matthew 2:5) and quoted this passage from Micah. Not only did the prophets promise the birth of the Messiah but also noted his place of birth. They recognized and understood the earlier references to the Messiah. The details of the promise were being filled out. Incidentally, David's father, Jesse, lived in Bethlehem.

Isaiah foresaw not only the coming of God's chosen or anointed one but also the resistance he would experience particularly from the religious and political leaders of the Jews. He appreciated the resolve and focus the Messiah would need to accomplish his mission. He also understood that throughout it all God would support and sustain him.

> Behold my servant, whom I uphold, my chosen, in whom my soul delights; I have put my Spirit upon him; he will bring forth justice to the nations. He will not cry aloud or lift up his voice, or make it heard in the streets; a bruised reed he will not break, and a faintly burning wick he will

not quench; he will faithfully bring forth justice.
He will not grow faint or be discouraged until he
has established justice in the earth; and the coast-
lands wait for his laws. (Isaiah 42:1–4)

This passage comments on the persistence that the Messiah will have to complete his mission despite the opposition he will face. He will not be broken or defeated, and his light will not be snuffed out. The light may flicker and dim but will not go out, and eventually, it will shine brilliantly for all to see. The Father will support him with the Holy Spirit throughout an incredibly difficult ordeal and finally accept his sacrifice and raise him to glory. As Jesus prepared to go to Jerusalem and the climax of his ministry, the *English Standard Version* of the Bible uses the term, "set his face to go," as does the *King James Version* to indicate his determination (Luke 9:51). The *New International Version* of the Bible uses the term *resolutely* which we may better understand. The promise is that he will single-mindedly accomplish his mission assigned by God.

That promise is expanded upon in Isaiah 49:1–7. Those verses make it clear that the servant is called and supported by God and that his work goes beyond the nation of Israel.

He [God] says: "It is to light a thing that you
should be my servant to raise up the tribes of Jacob
and to bring back the preserved of Israel; I will make
you as a light for the nations, that my salvation may
reach to the ends of the earth." (Isaiah 49:6)

You will recall that the twelve sons of Jacob were the forerunners of the tribes of Israel. Although the Messiah was to come from the Jews and to minister to them first, his disciples are to carry his message to the entire world. That is still an ongoing process and part of our responsibility as disciples of Christ.

The prophet Zechariah worked among the people who had returned from the Babylonian exile about 520 BC and after the new temple had been built in Jerusalem. He made several predictions and promises including foreseeing that despite opposition and resistance, the Messiah would enjoy some days of glory during his earthly ministry even though it may have been offered for the wrong reason.

> Rejoice greatly, O daughter of Zion! Shout
> aloud, O daughter of Jerusalem! Behold, your
> King is coming to you; righteous and having sal-
> vation is he, humble and mounted on a donkey,
> on a colt, the fold of a donkey. (Zechariah 9:9)

On the Sunday before his arrest and crucifixion, Jesus entered Jerusalem to the accolades of a large crowd that gathered along his way. It is uncertain whether most in the crowd truly understood his purpose or if they were still expecting the heroic and liberating Messiah. Is this the man that would cast off the Roman yoke and return Israel to its former glory? No matter the answer, the verses above were fulfilled.

> And those who went before and those who
> followed were shouting, "Hosanna! Blessed is he
> who comes in the name of the Lord! Blessed is the
> coming kingdom of our father David! Hosanna
> in the Highest!" (Mark 11:9–10)

Matthew also describes the event as the fulfillment of the prophet's promise and quotes the verse from Zechariah. From the height of this honored entry, things would rapidly go downhill to the very bottom of a dark valley on the following Friday.

Isaiah also graphically, and in some detail, lays out the suffering and death by crucifixion the Christ or the Messiah was to suffer.

> He was despised and rejected by men; a
> man of sorrows, and acquainted with grief, and
> as one from whom men hide their faces he was
> despised, and we esteemed him not. Surely he
> has borne our griefs and carried our sorrows; yet

we esteemed him stricken, smitten by God, and afflicted. But he was pierced for our transgressions; he was crushed for our iniquities; upon him was the chastisement that brought us peace, and with his wounds we are healed. All we like sheep have gone astray; we have turned—everyone—to his own way; and the LORD has laid on him the iniquity of us all. He was oppressed, and he was afflicted, yet he opened not his mouth; like a lamb that is led to the slaughter, and like a sheep that before its shearers is silent, so he opened not his mouth. (Isaiah 53:3–7)

The book of Psalms written by King David, King Solomon, and other religious leaders contains some amazing promises and descriptions of the *Passion* and crucifixion of the Messiah. Psalm 22 written by David is viewed as one of the most important of the messianic Psalms. It contains some of the most familiar verses of the Messiah's suffering and is quoted frequently in the New Testament. In verse 1, the Messiah cries out,

My God, my God, why have you forsaken me? Why are you so far from saving me, from the words of my groaning?

What is going on here? Why will God abandon the Messiah that he has long promised? How can this act lead to the formation of an everlasting kingdom? Verses 6 through 8 describe some of the ridicule and verbal abuse Jesus received from his brother Jews:

But I am a worm and not a man, scorned by mankind and despised by the people. All who see me mock me; they make mouths at me; they wag their heads; "He trusts in the Lord; let him deliver him; let him rescue him, for he delights in him!"

Versus 14 and 15 reveal some of the sufferings of his passion:

> I am poured out like water, and all my bones
> are out of joint; my heart is like wax; it is melted
> within my breast; my strength is dried up like a
> potsherd, and my tongue sticks to my jaws; you
> lay me in the dust of death.

Verses 16 to 18 describe the method of death by crucifixion and the distribution of his clothing by Roman soldiers:

> For dogs encompass me; a company of evil-
> doers encircles me; they have pierced my hands
> and feet—I can count all my bones—they stare
> and gloat over me; they divide my garments
> among them, and for my clothing they cast lots.

Not a very pretty picture of the torment and death of the Lord's anointed one. For what purpose?

The fulfillment of the Psalm 22 predictions and promises in the Gospels of the New Testament is remarkable. Matthew, Mark, Luke, and John each relate statements that Jesus made on the cross and of the verbal and physical abuse he endured. The entire ordeal from his arrest to his crucifixion is called the Lord's Passion. The Roman soldiers were anything but kind and inflicted brutal punishment and scorn prior to the crucifixion.

> And those who passed by derided him,
> wagging their heads and saying, "You who would
> destroy the temple and rebuild it in three days,
> save yourself! If you are the Son of God, come
> down from the cross." (Matthew 27:39–40)

As might be expected, the Roman soldiers charged with his crucifixion abused and mocked him, but even the scribes and priests got into the act. As was a common practice at the time, soldiers involved in such events often took the person's property as a supplement to their salary.

> And they crucified him and divided his
> garments among them, casting lots for them, to
> decide what each should take. (Mark 15:24)

John describes this event in a bit more detail and quotes the Isaiah passage in chapter 19 verses 23 and 24. John also reports that near the end of his ordeal, Jesus said that he was thirsty and was given sour wine on a sponge. That sounds a lot like he was dried out like a potsherd with his tongue sticking to his jaws.

Both Matthew and Mark record what perhaps is an astounding exclamation by Jesus from the cross.

> And about the ninth hour Jesus cried out
> with a loud voice, saying, "Eli, Eli, lema sabach-
> thani!" that is, "My God, my God, why have you
> forsaken me?" (Matthew 27:46)

Mark spells the first words *Eloi*; however, the meaning and message are the same. For Christians, this outcry may be confusing at first reading. How could God abandon Jesus at the time of his greatest need? To me, God's abandonment of Jesus is one of the most, if not the most, startling and sobering events of the entire Bible. It might seem cruel and confusing until we realize what is happening here. Here is the ultimate cost of the payment of our sins. The payment includes not only the physical and psychological pain but also the complete abandonment of Jesus by God so that we would not have to experience them.

Through Isaiah, God made another remarkable promise about the mission of the Messiah and what he would accomplish by his ministry on earth.

> He will swallow up death forever; and the
> LORD God will wipe away tears from all faces,

and the reproach of his people he will take away from all the earth, for the LORD has spoken. It will be said on that day, "Behold, this is our God; we have waited for him, that he might save us. This is the LORD; we have waited for him; let us be glad and rejoice in his salvation." (Isaiah 25:8–9)

How are we to understand this passage? Death has continued since Isaiah's day. In fact, it has continued since Jesus walked the earth and remains a reality. It produces feelings of loss and sadness, and we shed tears. We are heartbroken because life is not permanent. Yet this passage provides great comfort. Not only has the Lord promised to end death, but also he himself will wipe away our tears and bring us joy and salvation. For the believers of Isaiah's time, this was a forward-looking promise. For New Testament believers, this promise has been fulfilled and salvation assured. Mission accomplished!

Questions for Thought and Discussion

1. Read Isaiah 7:10–17. If you were a contemporary of the prophet Isaiah, would you have recognized verse 7:14 as a messianic prophecy? Perhaps consider some of the other Old Testament prophecies of a Messiah as well, such as Zachariah 11:12–13 and 13:1–7.
2. How did Isaiah's portrayal of the Messiah as a suffering servant conflict with the widely held concept of the Jews? How might it have influenced the acceptance of Jesus as the Messiah?
3. Compare Psalm 22:1 with Matthew 27:46. What is the significance of these verses?

New Testament Promises

But as it is, Christ has obtained a ministry that is as much
more excellent than the old as the covenant he mediates
is better, since it is enacted on better promises.
—Hebrews 8:6

In the passages of the New Testament Scriptures, God continued to promise his followers both temporal and eternal blessings. Often the promises are framed in such a way as to clarify, reaffirm, or explain the fulfillment of promises made in the Old Testament. As we have seen in the example of the centurion's servant shared earlier, the Son of God, Jesus, promised things that show us the benefits of our faith and how we are to apply them to our lives as Christians. One thing is true of the promises of both the Old and New Testaments: They originate from God, and they are good.

Do not be deceived, my beloved brothers.
Every good gift and every perfect gift is from
above, coming down from the Father of lights,
with whom there is no variation or shadow due
to change. (James 1:16–17)

We receive both temporal and eternal gifts through God's grace which is his love in action. Let's examine some of those promised gifts to understand what blessings they are for us and how we are to use them.

Promises of Temporal Blessings

As each has received a gift, use it to serve one another.

—1 Peter 4:10

Malachi, the last book of the Old Testament, was written about four hundred years before the birth of Jesus. After that, for a period of time, God appears to have been silent—no other prophets, no angelic messengers, no visions or dreams, at least none that were recorded until shortly before the birth of Jesus. The Gospels, written after he lived, most often identify Jesus as the direct source of important promises although some are provided by the authors of other books through inspiration. There were also some promises that were carried and delivered by heavenly messengers, that is angels or received in a dream or a vision.

God Promises Another Child

In this case, not the Christ child that you might be thinking of but rather a child who would grow up to take an active role in spreading the Gospel. Near the very end of Old Testament times, God promised an amazing event to a man named Zachariah just before Jesus was born. He was not the Old Testament prophet Zechariah but rather a priest serving in the temple in Jerusalem. Reminiscent of the promises made to the patriarchs Abraham and Isaac, God sent the angel Gabriel to tell Zechariah that he and his wife, Elizabeth, would be blessed with a child even though they were old.

> And Zachariah was troubled when he saw
> him, and fear fell upon him. But the angel said
> to him, "Do not be afraid, Zachariah, for your
> prayer has been heard, and your wife Elizabeth
> will bear you a son, and you shall call his name
> John. And you will have joy and gladness, and
> many will rejoice at his birth, for he will be great
> before the Lord." (Luke 1:12–15)

Fear is a common reaction when an angelic messenger confronted a human. Such fear is noted throughout the Bible and most often the first thing said by the holy messenger is, *"Fear not."* I shudder to think what my reaction would be if I was confronted by one of the heavenly messengers. The child promised to Zachariah and Elizabeth was the cousin of Jesus and his immediate forerunner, John the Baptist, whose call to repentance echoed throughout the land. This was more than a temporal promise to a childless couple. It contained an important eternal component as well. It was John who prepared the way for Jesus and preached the need for repentance. He baptized Jesus and pointed him out as the Lamb sent from God.

Jesus Promised Healing of Physical Diseases

For me, the highlights of the temporal promises in the Gospels are the healings performed by Jesus. Some of the promises of Jesus provided healing to those afflicted with various diseases and comfort to their family and friends. In some instances, the disease disappeared instantly while in others he instructed the recipient to obey a cultural requirement. For example, as Jesus was preaching in Galilee, a man with leprosy approached him and kneeling asked to be healed.

> Moved with pity, he stretched out his hand
> and touched him and said to him, "I will; be
> clean." And immediately the leprosy left him,
> and he was made clean. (Mark 1:41–42)

Later as Jesus was on his way to the fateful and historic events in Jerusalem, he encountered ten lepers who begged for his mercy.

> When he saw them he said to them, "Go
> and show yourselves to the priests." And as they
> went they were cleansed. (Luke 17:14)

They took the promise of their healing as fact and went to fulfill the requirement of their culture. Inspection by a priest had to occur before someone could be certified as clean of the disease. The interesting and disappointing thing about this event is that only one of the ten returned to give thanks to Jesus for being healed. Despite the fulfillment of his promise and being healed, the rest showed indifference if not ingratitude as we humans often do. How many times have we prayed, received our request, and moved along without remembering to give thanks?

On another occasion, Jesus was back in Cana, the site of his first miracle of turning water into wine probably during his trip to Galilee referred to above. There an official from the city of Capernaum spoke to him and requested that he come and heal his son who was dying. Jesus again responded positively to the man's request and promised healing.

> Jesus said to him, "Go; your son will live."
> The man believed the word that Jesus spoke to
> him and went on his way. (John 4:50)

As the man was on his way home, he was met by one of his servants who told him that his son was well. Another encouragement for us to believe his words. The lesson that we learn again from the examples of the lepers and the official is to have faith and go.

Jesus has been called the great physician, but he is not called that in the Bible. These examples are only two of the many reported in the Gospels. Most probably, he healed many more than have been recorded. His miraculous healings came from his great compassion for the suffering of people, but they also were done with a purpose.

Beyond demonstrating his divine power, they taught his disciples empathy for others, to be thankful for gifts, and to produce witnesses of his ministry. Think of the joy and excitement with which the father spread the news of his child's healing. Even the nine ungrateful lepers must eventually have valued their cure and passed on the news. Jesus has not promised to heal all our diseases and injuries, but I believe he can and has cured many at his discretion. Compassion, gratitude, and witnessing our blessings are excellent lessons for us to learn.

God Promises Comfort

God's comfort is not the creature comforts that many of us enjoy especially at this time in our great nation. When things really go bad in our lives, and all seems to be crashing down upon us, those things provide little solace. We look to be consoled and comforted. Family members, friends, counselors, and pastors can provide us with loving support and insights that help us to understand and deal with our troubles. At such times, God's Word provides lasting solace if we turn to it and listen to its message.

> Now may our Lord Jesus Christ himself,
> and God our Father, who loved us and gave us
> eternal comfort and good hope through grace,
> comfort your hearts and establish them in every
> good work and word. (2 Thessalonians 2:16–17)

God promises to comfort us and lift us up so that we can go on with our lives. But there is more to it than that. Times of trials can be learning experiences through which we not only are comforted but are prepared to extend loving concern and comfort to others when they are experiencing their own problems.

> Blessed be the God and Father of our Lord
> Jesus Christ, the Father of mercies and God of all
> comfort, who comforts us in all our affliction, so
> that we may be able to comfort those who are in

> any affliction, with the comfort with which we
> ourselves are comforted by God. (2 Corinthians
> 1:3–4)

God not only promises and provides comfort to us but also expects and even directs that we will pass it on. We misunderstand our role as Christians if we receive and accept comfort but neglect or ignore another person in need of a kind word or a helping hand.

God Promises to Never Leave Us

As humans, we each have needs, wants, and desires in our daily lives. Most often, we have more wants and desires than needs. It seems to be a human characteristic to look for more and more things to enrich our lives and make us more comfortable. For example, note the TV and print commercials for health insurance that encourage us to call to make sure that we receive all the benefits that we deserve or to which we are entitled. Still better we can get them with little or no cost to us. Other commercials announce phenomenal sales of all types of articles with the advice, "The more you spend the more you save!" It seems that we are always striving to get all there is to get and yet are not satisfied. We are trying to keep up with the Joneses, who are trying to keep up with the Smiths, who are trying to keep up with someone else. There is always more to get that will make us happy. We are sure what will make us happy is whatever we don't have.

On the other hand, God has given us some advice about this condition and also tacked a promise to it.

> Keep your life free from love of money, and be
> content with what you have, for he has said, "I will
> never leave you nor forsake you." (Hebrews 13:5)

The author of the book of Hebrews here restates a promise made to the Israelites in Joshua 1:5. God reinforced that promise in Psalm 37 with a passage that sounds surprisingly like those of the New Testament.

> For the LORD loves justice; he will not for-
> sake his saints. They are preserved forever, but
> the children of the wicked shall be cut off. (Psalm
> 37:28)

He will be with us throughout our lives if we have faith in Jesus. It has been said that it is not important to get what we want but rather to want what we get. That sounds like good advice especially in the light of God's promise never to forsake us if we follow him.

God Promises Help for Our Anxious Lives

In this time of head-spinning change, economic uncertainties, worldwide political entanglements, and climate questions, things are confused at best and perhaps chaotic. What are we to believe? Who are we to trust? How do we handle all this? There seems to be plenty to worry about.

Beyond our health and the health of our loved ones, most of us have some concerns about the permanency of our job and our paycheck. What do we do if our job is eliminated because the company is downsizing, moving, or going out of business? What happens to our house or car if we can no longer afford to keep up the payments, and how do we cope without them? Our dreams of a secure and comfortable retirement may vanish as the stock market falls or our other investments turn out to have been bad choices. How will our children be able to afford a college education or advanced training? What can we do when our aging parents need assistance? Will we be able to afford even basic necessities? Is there a major war on the horizon and can it be averted? Is another pandemic inevitable as infectious bacteria and viruses become more resistant to our drugs? How will our culture and the way we live be impacted by the development of artificial intelligence?

There are more than enough concerns to make us uneasy and even suspicious. These nagging thoughts and questions can result in sleepless nights and an upset stomach if not real ulcers. A little reassurance and support here would be appreciated.

True to form, our great God has given us an antidote for our anxieties. Jesus addressed these issues when speaking to his disciples. He said,

> Therefore I tell you, do not be anxious about your life, what you will eat or what you will drink, nor about your body, what you will put on. Is not life more than food, and the body more than clothing? Look at the birds of the air: they neither sow nor reap nor gather into barns, and yet your heavenly Father feeds them. Are you not of more value than they? (Matthew 6:25–33)

Furthermore, he went on to provide some important advice about priorities in our lives.

> For all the nations of the world seek after these things, and your Father knows that you need them. Instead seek his kingdom, and these things will be added to you. (Luke 12:30–31)

There is much more to say about promises of the kingdom coming up.

Our Gifts and Their Use

As disciples of Christ, we all have been given gifts that we can and should use in his service. Some can fix or build almost anything. They have the ability to provide invaluable service to the congregation and to others in the community who might need assistance. They do the hard and often unappreciated things for the congregation that keep the lights on and the doors open, the walks shoveled, and the grass cut. They also are able to use their skills to assist members of the community at large in ways that directly impact their quality of life or spiritual well-being.

Some of us are good administrators and can organize and guide the affairs of our congregation or other organizations effectively. Others can preach or teach the Word to people of various ages from the very young to the very old. They can speak with clarity and force and can inspire people to apply their gifts as well. The members of praise teams and choirs, organists, and pianists inspire us with their musical talents and add so much to our worship services. There are those who are great encouragers who provide support when someone is experiencing loneliness or loss. Artistic folks help to design new buildings or additions, with decorating the church, and preparing materials for ministry programs and courses. The list could go on, for there are many more specific skills that we have. No one has all the skills and talents that sustain the message of the Gospel. Instead, each forms a critical part of the whole.

> As each has received a gift, use it to serve one another, as good stewards of God's varied grace: whoever speaks, as one who speaks oracles of God; whoever serves, as one who serves by the strength that God supplies—in order that in everything God may be glorified through Jesus Christ. To him belong glory and dominion forever and ever. Amen. (1 Peter 4:10–11)

We are promised and have received talents and abilities. It is an important point to remember the source of those gifts. We had little if anything to do with acquiring our gifts; they are truly from God, but we have a lot to do with how we use those gifts to serve.

Questions for Thought and Discussion

1. Which of the temporal blessings found in the New Testament do you feel is most important or meaningful to you personally?
2. Local, state, and federal agencies as well as private organizations are beginning to realize and are addressing men-

tal health issues as they pertain to the mass murders and homelessness problems. However, little effort seems to be directed toward eliminating the underlying causes. In your opinion, why are so many people experiencing mental health issues and becoming violent as a result?

3. Thinking about your gifts both personal and material, when did you realize that they were just that, gifts, and not from your own hard work?

Eternal Promises

Let us hold fast the confession of our hope without wavering,
for he who promised is faithful.
—Hebrews 10:23

As he did in the Old Testament, God promises his disciples eternal blessings in the New Testament. In addition, he provides fulfillment of those Old Testament promises. We have already seen how he promised many times to send a Messiah to save us and then fulfilled that promise through the birth, ministry, crucifixion, and resurrection of Jesus. That is the point; all the promises are founded on Jesus.

God Promises Mercy

The passage in Second Corinthians quoted earlier also contains another significant and eternal promise in the words "the father of mercies." Quite often, when I was a boy, my frustrated mother would say to me when she had enough of my shenanigans, "Now, you are really going to get it when your father gets home." Most times I got what I deserved, but once in a while, my dad relented, and I received mercy. God is the great purveyor of mercy and as faith-filled Christians, we always receive it. We should note here that this is not the promise that we will not be harmed during our daily lives and the difficult situations in which we might find ourselves but rather that we are safe for eternity. God sent his son Jesus Christ to be the *propitiation* for our sins. Because God imputed our sins to Christ, and likewise his righteousness to us, our debt has been paid, and we are set free. We no longer are in danger of eternal punishment. Thankfully, God carried out his promise that came down through the Old Testament prophets. The Gentiles are included in his kingdom.

> Once you were not a people, but now you are God's people; once you had not received mercy, but now you have received mercy. (1 Peter 2:10)

Hallelujah! We are not shut out! We are not going to get it! The cross that we see in our church or wear around our neck is a symbol of that reality and should remind us of the tremendous cost of our salvation. This is a promise of mercy on a grand scale.

God Promises Help When We Are Tempted

Just as with God's people of the Old Testament, temptations seem to be everywhere in these modern times. Opportunities to take part in less than God-pleasing activities are frequent and look so satisfying, even harmless. Why do they always seem to play to our weaknesses? We may be tempted to overclaim a financial loss or fail to report fully a financial gain. A little slacking at the office or pilfering from the supply cabinet is not really a bad thing, and besides, the company makes so much money. We can so easily be seduced by money, sex, drugs, drinks, knowledge, power, and even friendship. Perhaps, we consider temptation to be only a temporal weakness that results in legal problems or the loss of respect and reputation in our day-to-day life. However, temptations can lead us into a lifestyle that is anything but Christian and the loss of our faith.

As it is with innovation, so it is with temptation; there is nothing truly new under the sun. When we are tempted, we face a choice between giving in or resisting and doing the right thing. Although we are not good at resisting temptation alone, there is help available. Good Christian spouses, friends, and pastors who will tell us when we were heading in the wrong direction are invaluable to help us stand up and resist. Difficult as it may be, resistance is possible. God has promised that we can stand up and do the right thing with his help.

> No temptation has overcome you that is not common to man. God is faithful, and he will not let you be tempted beyond your ability, but with the temptation he will also provide the way of escape, that you may be able to endure it. (1 Corinthians 10:13)

We need to ask God to strengthen us, show us the way of escape, and keep us steadfast in the faith as we struggle each day with our own weaknesses.

We Are Promised Access to God the Father

Here is one that many of us do not value as highly as we should. It is called prayer. We have been assured that we can approach God the Father directly. Because of the sacrifice of Jesus, we no longer have the need for an intermediary. We no longer require someone else to offer a sacrifice in our stead. No priest is needed to carry our requests to heaven.

> For through him we both (Jews and Gentiles) have access in one Spirit to the Father. (Ephesians 2:18)

Martin Luther called this "the priesthood of all believers." The direct line is open and all calls, no matter how trivial or how important, are welcome and receive an answer. No matter what we ask in Jesus's name, we will receive a hearing.

> My little children, I am writing these things to you so that you may not sin. But if anyone does sin, we have an advocate with the Father, Jesus Christ the righteous. (1 John 2:1)

Even when we badly mess up, Jesus is there to say to the Father, "Remember what I did. For my sake hear that prayer." Because Jesus promised several times to hear us, we tend to think of this as a unique New Testament promise; however, in the Old Testament, God also promised to hear the prayers of his children.

> The LORD is near to all who call on him, to
> all who call on him in truth. He fulfills the desire
> of those who fear him; he also hears their cry and
> saves them. (Psalm 145:18–19)

We are encouraged to pray often, and the more we use it, the stronger our relationship with God becomes; our confidence grows, and our comfort is increased.

> Rejoice always, pray without ceasing, give
> thanks in all circumstances; for this is the will
> of God in Christ Jesus for you. (1 Thessalonians
> 5:16–18)

Some of you might remember the popular TV program, *Frazier*, a spinoff from another program, *Cheers*. Frazier was a psychiatrist in Seattle who had a radio call-in show. On the show, he would provide counseling and personal advice to listeners who contacted him on the phone. When someone called with a problem, he would address them saying, "This is Dr. Fraser Crane. Go ahead. I'm listening." Many of the problems and much of the advice were comedic of course, but Frazier seriously sought to help people. However, he was only listening to those people while he was on the air. In contrast, God is always on the line. Just open the line and connect with the Father. He is always listening.

God Promises Peace

Peace is another gift from God. But let's not misunderstand the peace we are talking about because there seems to be a conflict. Paul uses the word in the greetings of most of his epistles, and the angels used it in their announcement of the birth of Jesus. Jesus himself often after healing someone sent them on their way saying, "Go in peace." Paul encourages his readers,

> If possible, so far as it depends on you, live
> peaceably with all. (Romans 12:18)

The author of the book of Hebrews says much the same thing.

> Strive for peace with everyone, and for the
> holiness without which no one will see the Lord.
> (Hebrews 12:14)

Certainly, as Christians, we should attempt to live harmoniously with everyone, particularly with our brothers and sisters of faith.

But wait! We know that the world is anything but peaceful. Crimes are frequent and often brutal, altercations between individuals happen every day, groups scrimmage and riot violently, and wars between nations seem to be constant. Mass murderers occur much too often. It doesn't seem that things are getting better. Even within our congregations or social groups, it is so easy to become upset with other members and feel anything but peace in their presence. Jesus warned about his ministry and its effects.

> Do you think that I have come to give peace
> on earth? No, I tell you, but rather a division.
> (Luke 12:51)

He then goes on to explain that even families will be divided by his message. Members will be set against each other because some will have faith and believe while others will not. Some will treasure the Gospel while others will ridicule it. How peaceful is it when our faith results in strained or broken relationships with family members, friends, and colleagues.

So where is this peace we are promised, and how do we obtain it? Thank God, we already have it. We don't have to search for it. We don't have to work for it. We don't have to pay for it. We just have to have faith in the one who earned it for us and promises it to us as a gift. Yes, peace is personal to each of us, but more so, it depends on one person.

> Therefore, since we have been justified by faith, we have peace with God through our Lord Jesus Christ. (Romans 5:1)

We are not talking about cordial relationships among acquaintances nor the shaky treaties of peace between nations. This is eternal peace between God and humans won for us by the blood of Jesus on the cross. It is a peace that is so vitally important to us yet beyond our understanding.

God Promise of Eternal Life and More!

We have been promised mercy from God, peace with God, and direct access to God. What is the bottom line of all these remarkable promises? So what more can there be? What does this all mean to us or for us? Most assuredly, these are promises of the first magnitude. Peter has the answers to these questions and clearly lays them out for us.

> His divine power has granted to us all things that pertain to life and godliness, through the knowledge of him who called us to his own glory and excellence, by which he has granted to us his precious and very great promises, so that through them you may become partakers of the divine nature, having escaped from the corruption that is in the world because of sinful desire. (2 Peter 1:3–4)

Because of Christ, we are given the power to take on a divine nature. What does that mean? Simply, we have been granted forgiveness of our sins, considered righteous, and therefore through faith have eternal life.

> And this is the promise that he made to
> us—eternal life. (1 John 2:25)

That is quite a promise. It is hope fulfilled!

Sometimes the fulfillment of that promise is startlingly direct and immediate. When one of the two thieves being crucified at the same time expressed faith in him, Jesus replied,

> And he [Jesus] said to him, "Truly, I say
> to you, today you will be with me in paradise."
> (Luke 23:43)

This shakes us and makes us take notice. A man dying for his sins, particularly those committed against the Roman Empire, is granted a pardon. Jesus has the power not only to forgive sins but also to confer a place in paradise. On what basis did this man called a thief receive forgiveness and eternal life, and more importantly for us, how do we receive the same reward? Is it by following the law and living a good Christian life? Obviously, this was not the case for the man next to Jesus on the cross, for he was a lawbreaker, and so are we.

> For all who rely on works of the law are
> under a curse; for it is written, "Cursed be every-
> one who does not abide by all things written in
> the Book of the Law, and do them." (Galatians
> 3:10)

The answer: by the grace of God through faith in Jesus Christ. Believers of the Old Testament time looked forward to a Savior coming under the guardianship of the Law. New Testament believers look backward to the cross and the completed mission of Jesus Christ.

> But now that faith has come, we are no
> longer under a guardian, for in Christ Jesus you
> are all sons of God, through faith. (Galatians
> 3:25–26)

Perhaps in this time of political correctness, some would argue that this passage should say, "The sons and daughters" or "children," but nevertheless the meaning is clear; gender does not matter nor do self-selected pronouns. The promise is to those of faith and that matters greatly. The lesson here: Have faith and be saved.

What could be more than the gift of eternal life? Well, here it is. There is frosting on this beautiful cake. We like to think of ourselves as servants of Jesus. But we are actually considered more than that. We are also considered his friends. In the fifteenth chapter of John, Jesus is speaking of the great love of someone who is willing to die for someone else and commands us to love each other. I am sure that he was thinking of his soon to occur death on the cross for us and continued with a remarkable statement.

> No longer do I call you servants, for the
> servant does not know what his master is doing;
> but I have called you friends, for all that I have
> heard from my Father I have made known to
> you. (John 15:15)

What a promise that is to be called a friend of Jesus.

But there is still more. It is not unusual to hear a pastor or other speakers address a congregation or a group as "brothers and sisters in Christ" as a term of identification and unity. Actually, it is even better than that. The author of the book of Hebrews commenting about the founder of our salvation writes,

> For he who sanctifies and those who are
> sanctified all have one source. That is why he
> is not ashamed to call them brothers. (Hebrews
> 2:11)

Amazing! By God's grace, we have eternal life as his children through faith in Christ who calls us friends and his brothers and sisters. These are ultra-sweet promises.

The Promises of the Resurrection of Jesus

Jesus had predicted his death and promised his resurrection several times which dismayed and confused his disciples. They were unable to grasp how his death could fulfill the law and the writings of the prophets and accomplish his purpose. The writers of the four gospels record at least three separate instances in which he addressed that issue. That thought was so distasteful that the ever-forceful Peter stated that he would never let that happen to the Christ. They had not grasped the significance of what was about to happen. Perhaps they just could not face the reality of his death. In fact, on the trip to Jerusalem just before his betrayal and arrest, they were still disputing who would be the greatest among them in the coming kingdom of God. They had understood the prediction and feared its fulfillment but had missed or misunderstood the promise that Jesus had connected with it.

> For he was teaching his disciples, saying to them, "The Son of Man is going to be delivered into the hands of men, and they will kill him. And when he is killed, after three days he will rise." But they did not understand the saying, and were afraid to ask him. (Mark 9:31–32)

That Thursday evening when Jesus was arrested and hauled away to stand trial before the Sanhedrin, their greatest fears were realized. The prediction was about to come to fruition, and it became a night of darkness, denial, and dispersion. On Sunday morning, the resurrection was a fact, and the light of understanding began to glow but dimly. They came to realize just how important the promise was, for without its fulfillment, all would be lost for them and for us. Jesus comforted and strengthened them over a period of forty days before he was taken back to heaven.

The resurrection has been questioned and disbelieved by many. They have sought and advanced many explanations other than those in the words of the Scriptures. Here are some. Jesus was a twin. One was crucified, and the other took his place to lead the disciples. I know that twins are extremely devoted to each other willing to donate organs to the ailing sibling and even to take action to save the other from a dangerous situation. However, to agree to construct an elaborate hoax in which one dies an excruciating death seems more than far-fetched. Another suggests that the disciples somehow were able to steal Jesus's body and spirit it away into hiding. They then spread the story of the empty tomb and the resurrection to inspire their followers and themselves into lives filled with beatings, imprisonment, and painful death. I can't imagine a more unlikely scenario.

An interesting idea is that the Roman soldiers took pity on Jesus and helped him to avoid crucifixion. Several weaknesses exist in this explanation. First, Roman soldiers were not known for their sensitivity and compassion, and besides they had just finished flogging, beating, and belittling him. Second, who was the man who died on the third cross? No! A hoax, a stolen body, or helpful Roman soldiers would not have affected those men in such a way. Something extremely life-changing happened starting them on a path that led most of them to martyrs' deaths. However, they were not confident in themselves and needed additional strength and assurance to move on. It was soon to be supplied in a most dramatic fashion!

The Promise of the Holy Spirit

But there's even more. When Jesus left the disciples and ascended into heaven, they again must have felt loss and uncertainty. Although they had been trained and partially prepared to take on the ministry, they realized that they could not succeed on their own. Several times Jesus had tried to reassure them and promised to send a helper who would not only strengthen them but would also assist them to persevere through the difficult days ahead.

These things I have spoken to you while I am still with you. But the Helper, the Holy Spirit, whom the Father will send in my name, he will teach you all things and bring to your remembrance all that I have said to you. (John 14:25–26)

Not only did Jesus promise that God the Father would send the Holy Spirit, but he also promised that they would receive a full understanding of what he had taught them. We sometimes wonder how it was that the disciples did not fully appreciate and understand the promises and explanations. How could they not grasp the importance of what he told them? I believe that part of the answer lies in the fact that what Jesus was teaching was so different than their previous religious practices. No longer was a tradition-bound, sacrifice-based, and priestly controlled procedure necessary in which the people stood outside in the temple courtyards while inside, the priests offered sacrifices for their sins. He was revealing that people individually could approach God through faith in him.

Now it was time for the promises of the Holy Spirit to be fulfilled. As remarkable as the promises were, their fulfillment was more so. Following his crucifixion, Jesus appeared to his disciples several times and again promised that they would receive the Holy Spirit.

And while staying with them he ordered them not to depart from Jerusalem, but to wait for the promise of the Father, which, he said, "you heard from me; for John baptized with water, but You will be baptized with the Holy Spirit not many days from now." (Acts 1:4–5)

The disciples must have been thinking, *What does it mean to be baptized with the Holy Spirit?* Sometime later at his ascension as he left them for the final time, he provided them with an indication of what the gift of the promised Spirit would mean for them.

> But you will receive power when the Holy
> Spirit has come upon you, and you will be my
> witnesses in Jerusalem and in all Judea and
> Samaria, and to the ends of the earth. (Acts 1:8)

Being powerful witnesses was probably the last thing on the disciples' minds as they waited behind locked doors. Though they had seen the risen Savior and had received further teaching from him, they were still unsteady and in need of assurance. They were about to receive it in a most astounding way.

Slowly the apostles were growing in their faith and becoming more confident as they understood the significance of the resurrection and the ascension. Then an amazing event happened.

> When the date of Pentecost arrived, they
> were all together in one place. And suddenly
> there came from heaven a sound like a mighty
> rushing wind, and it filled the entire house where
> they were sitting. And divided tongues as of fire
> appeared to them and rested on each one of them.
> And they were all filled with the Holy Spirit and
> began to speak in other tongues as the Spirit gave
> them utterance. (Acts 2:1–4)

Here was the fulfillment of the promise with the power of the Holy Spirit vividly displayed (Appendix 4). This was a transformative experience that was badly needed by a group of timid men that turned them into outspoken witnesses of the faith. It emboldened them to begin the spread of the Gospel that continues to this day.

How are we to understand this miraculous event and the change in character and behavior it produced? As with the resurrection, it has been questioned and ridiculed by many. Even at the time, the apostles were accused of being under the influence of alcohol. Things have not gotten better with the passage of time.

So what does the Holy Spirit do? The Spirit is the one who initiates and grows the faith of sinful human beings. He opens the doors that turn the sinner from a path that leads to destruction to one that leads to faith in Jesus Christ and salvation. Just as Jesus told the apostles, the Spirit brings us a deeper understanding and appreciation of the Scriptures and the power to do more than we ever thought possible. When things are in turmoil and our thoughts are chaotic, we may find it difficult to form a coherent prayer to the Father. We may be experiencing deep grief, great fear, overwhelming circumstances, or deep emotion. It is at that point that the Holy Spirit steps in and helps us.

> Likewise the Spirit helps us in our weakness. For we do not know what to pray for as we ought, but the Spirit himself intercedes for us with groanings too deep for words. And he who searches hearts knows what is the mind of the Spirit, because the Spirit intercedes for the saints according to the will of God. (Romans 8:26–27)

I would venture to say that most of us do not pray as well, as often, or as effectively as we could and should. I know that I don't. It is so easy to be distracted as we pray or to dash off a short thoughtless prayer. Even at such times of carelessness or when we are under stress, the Holy Spirit is there with us to ensure that our prayers reach the Father in the proper way.

The Spirit is not only with us when we seem to feel his presence. When we are singing a rousing song, hearing a forceful sermon, or attending a large rally of loud excited Christians, we feel elated. But his presence does not depend on our feelings. The room may not be shaking, but nevertheless, he is always with us as the promised Helper. That is extremely good news. Because if we give up on the Spirit during times of misfortune, sadness, or temptation, we forfeit much of the comfort and help that we need to navigate the complexities of life and perhaps lose the hope of eternal life as well.

Questions for Thought and Discussion

1. Do you believe that the apostles and the other disciples of Christ could have been deceived about his resurrection? For you, what is the strongest evidence that the resurrection actually occurred?
2. Read 1 Corinthians 15:12–19. Do you agree with Paul's comments? Explain.
3. How is our interaction and relationship with God different than that of the believers of the Old Testament?
4. God has promised us peace in our lives. Do you ever feel anything but peaceful in your life or your relationship with God?

Promises of Persecution and Hardship

Do not be surprised, brothers, that the world hates you.
—1 John 3:13

Whoa! The passage above is startling and unsettling. Does the world hate us, the disciples of Jesus? Why? Despite all the good things promised, God does not guarantee a carefree life of fun and games for his disciples. In fact, shortly after the fall, he had some less than cordial words for Adam and Eve, and for us.

To the woman he said, "I will surely multiply your pain in childbearing; in pain you shall bring forth children. Your desire shall be for your husband, and he shall rule over you." (Genesis 3:16)

He did not let Adam off the hook either.

By the sweat of your face you shall eat bread, till you return to the ground, for out of it you were taken; for you are dust, and to dust you shall return. (Genesis 3:19)

Beyond that, however, we experience all the disappointments, losses, setbacks, diseases, and disasters that humans are subject to. When such things overtake us and perhaps overwhelm us, we can respond in many ways. We can break down, give up, and curse our bad luck. We might revile against God, accusing him of being the cause of our problems and not caring for us. We will then live out our life in frustration and anger. We can acquiesce meekly and accept our lot and continue to make our way aimlessly through life. Painful childbirth, hard work, sickness, and troubles? That's not what most of us would like to have. That is not what we signed up for. This life is not a cakewalk for the weak. Who needs that anyway? The answer is we do to remind us of our inherited sinful condition and to whom we need to look to endure.

There is another way to respond. We can accept our troubles whatever they might be and ask God to give us strength and direction to persevere.

> Not only that, but we rejoice in our sufferings, knowing that suffering produces endurance, and endurance produces character, and character produces hope, and hope does not put us to shame, because God's love has been poured out into our hearts through the Holy Spirit who has been given to us. (Romans 5:3–5)

Hard words to live by? Maybe. To be joyful in our suffering is certainly challenging for most of us. But here's the promise: God is always ready to help if we humbly ask according to his will and in the name of his son, Jesus. In a discussion with a group of friends asking her about the state of her cancer diagnosis, treatment, and prognosis, a wise woman said, "I can't lose either way. Either I become better, or I become perfect." My wife is always saying things like that. Bless her soul.

The second verse of the hymn ("What a friend we have in Jesus") provides some solid advice for dealing with our problems. It says, "Have we trials and temptations? Is there trouble anywhere? We should never be discouraged. Take it to the Lord in prayer. Can we find a friend so faithful Who will all our sorrows share? Jesus knows our every weakness. Take it to the Lord in prayer." Great advice!

The Cost of Discipleship

Jesus issued some sobering warnings during his ministry. Over the years, many bad things have happened to believers that have resulted in a loss of reputation, position, fortune, friendships, and even torture and death. Jesus warned his disciples and particularly the apostles that following him would have its costs. They would not be exempt from the same kind of treatment that he received from his contemporaries. It has been said again by a proverbial someone, "Salvation is free but discipleship is not;" it comes with a cost. While relating a series of stern warnings to his apostles, Jesus said,

> "But all these things they will do to you on
> account of my name, because they do not know
> him who sent me." (John 15:21)

So there it is. There is the reason. They don't believe Jesus, and they don't know God the Father.

Paul, the great apostle and missionary to the Gentiles, was no exception or exempt from hardships. After Jesus's resurrection and ascension, he made a promise in a most astounding way to Paul then known as the Pharisee Saul who was at the time persecuting the fledgling Christian church. As he was traveling to Damascus, he was confronted by the risen Jesus in a vision.

> And falling to the ground he [Saul] heard
> a voice saying to him, "Saul, Saul, why are you
> persecuting me?" And he said, "Who are you,
> Lord?" And he said, "I am Jesus who you are per-
> secuting." (Acts 9:4–5)

Temporarily blind for three days, he was led into the city where a man named Ananias was told to seek Saul out. Ananias hesitated for he well knew Saul's reputation.

> But the Lord said to him, "Go, for he is a
> chosen instrument of mine to carry my name
> before the Gentiles and the Kings and the chil-
> dren of Israel." (Acts 9:15)

By that, Saul was converted, renamed Paul, and made an apostle of Jesus. Yet he cautioned the Christians of the first century and
also us of the twenty-first century that evil might not be punished in
this lifetime.

> Indeed, all who desire to live a godly life
> in Christ Jesus will be persecuted, while evil
> people and impostors will go on from bad to
> worse, deceiving and being deceived. (2 Timothy
> 3:12–13)

In several places, he listed the troubles he endured for preaching
the Gospel. He was beaten, driven out of town, shipwrecked, imprisoned, and finally executed. Nevertheless, Paul always considered his
conversion and the promise that he would become a great missionary
to the Gentiles to be the greatest gift of his life. It may not be fair,
and we may be wronged, but life is very often an unfair adventure.
Despite that, we are safe in Jesus.

Jesus sought to prepare his disciples for what they were to face
after he leaves them. The authorities, Jewish and Roman, will not be
kind to them and will try to suppress their message sometimes with
violent actions. Despite the opposition and difficulties they will face,
he wanted to assure them that they will have success and obtain a
reward if they persevere.

> And you will be hated by all for my name's
> sake. But the one who endures to the end will be
> saved. (Mark 13:13)

Here is a warning of future difficulties hooked onto a promise
of a good ending. But the ending might be a long time away down

a difficult road. Faith, trust, patience, and perseverance are in order here. Shortly after Jesus ascended and following the outpouring of the Holy Spirit on Pentecost, the apostles were emboldened to speak in public about the good news and their faith in Jesus.

Peter and John were arrested and brought before the Sanhedrin, the Jewish council. They were charged not to speak or teach in the name of Jesus and released. That was an unacceptable demand, and they continued to teach the people in public. Arrested a second time and imprisoned, they were freed from their cells by an angel. The following morning, they went to the temple to continue to teach and were brought before the Sanhedrin again. The members did not know quite what to do with them because they were popular with the people. Then a Pharisee named Gamaliel counseled that the members of the Sanhedrin should be temperate in their response to the apostles. He advised that if the teaching was man-made, it would fail, but if it was from God, they could not stop it and might even be opposing God. This time, they were beaten and again charged not to teach in the name of Jesus.

There is another cost of discipleship that might be more disheartening and painful than that which we receive from the world around us. Strained or broken relationships with family members, friends, and colleagues might result because of our faith and discipleship. Those disruptions are especially hard to accept, they are among the bitterest of pills to swallow and may never be resolved as we may hope.

The Purpose of Troubles

So why were the apostles subjected to this type of treatment and even more severe methods in the years to come when some were martyred? Was there some reason that these men were so cruelly handled, or was it only to prevent them from enjoying a soft and comfortable life? After all, weren't they apostles of the Son of God, and shouldn't that mean that the road would be an easy one? Jesus had provided the reason while he was with them. It was to provide them with opportunities to witness to powerful leaders and to other people beyond Israel.

> Beware of men, for they will deliver you over to the courts and flog you in their synagogues, and you will be dragged before governors and kings for my sake, to bear witness before them and the Gentiles. (Matthew 10:17–18)

For most of us in the United States, being a witness to the Gospel is not fraught with severe danger. We might be subject to some disapproval or discrimination where we work or study. We might experience comments about how closed-minded we are or how far out of date our beliefs are. We might be ignored, insulted, or shouted down when we speak about our Savior. But few of us experience real danger or injuries. Nevertheless, we often fail to stand up and effectively defend our beliefs. Yet God promised to assist the apostles specifically and also to help us in our efforts.

> And when they bring you before the synagogues and the rulers and the authorities, do not be anxious about how you should defend yourself or what you should say, for the Holy Spirit will teach you in that very hour what you ought to say. (Luke 12:11–12)

The Lord directed their attention as he does ours to the promised helper, the Holy Spirit. We will be given words in those instances. They may not always be elegant and smoothly delivered but they will be the right words. We are not responsible for the ultimate effect of those words; the Holy Spirit is; we are responsible to deliver them.

We are actually blessed when we take advantage of those opportunities to witness for Christ no matter how unprepared we may feel or how we may be received. Even when we experience disdain or rejection, we must take advantage of those instances to express our faith. And God has given us another promise. It is another *if/then* promise.

> So everyone who acknowledges me before men, I also will acknowledge before my Father who is in heaven, but whoever denies me before men, I also will deny before my Father who is in heaven. (Matthew 10:32–33)

We will be blessed and rewarded in heaven if we do so and disowned if we do not. I am unsure just how we will be rewarded beyond receiving the gift of eternal life in heaven, but a number of passages such as Psalm 62:12, Jeremiah 32:19, Matthew 5:11–12, and Luke 6:22–23 seem to speak to that subject. These passages also tell us to rejoice when we receive opposition when we express our faith in Christ. With our easily bruised egos, that might prove even more difficult than dealing with personal troubles and adversities.

Questions for Thought and Discussion

1. Do you believe that there are different rewards in heaven? If so, why and how do you see them?
2. Have you ever felt personal persecution of any type? Specifically, when, why, and what kind?
3. Jesus said, "Ask and you shall receive." How do you rectify that with the times you have not received your request?
4. Is it difficult for you to remain thankful and joyful when times are difficult and bad things are happening? How do you manage?

The Final Promise

Surely I am coming soon.

—Revelation 22:20

During his time on earth, as Jesus taught his disciples and ministered to the people, he made many promises, all of which have been fulfilled except one. He calls us friends and brothers and sisters whom he will never forsake and provides us peace, comfort, an antidote for anxiety, and strength in times of trouble or temptation. He has given each of us our personal gifts and talents, and innumerable blessings of all types. He has obtained, including for us, Gentiles, direct access to the Father, freedom from the curse of the law, and mercy so that we need not pay the debt of sin that we owe. Indeed, he has promised us salvation and eternal life.

You might argue that the promise of eternal life has not actually been fulfilled. However, his promised resurrection and ascension have occurred and are proof that his sacrifice has been accepted by God the Father thereby assuring that our hope of eternal life is already fulfilled. His promise to send the Holy Spirit occurred on Pentecost. He also promised that his disciples would not lead a carefree life but would experience all the normal human difficulties and troubles and that some would experience ridicule, persecution, and even death. All these have been fulfilled in one way or another. Yet there is one promise that is still open.

The Unfulfilled Promise

So what is this last and final promise that has not happened? It is a promise that literally will turn the world upside down when the time comes for it to be fulfilled. It is the day of the Lord, Judgment Day, when Christ will return. Believers and unbelievers alike will tremble on that day, but for believers, it will turn to joy while for unbelievers, it will be a day of destruction. The day of the Lord is mentioned a number of times in the Old Testament. Some 430 years before the birth of Jesus, the prophet Malachi wrote,

> Behold, I send my messenger, and he will prepare the way before me. And the LORD whom you seek will suddenly come to his temple; and the messenger of the covenant in whom you delight, behold, he is coming, says the LORD of hosts. But who can endure the day of his coming, and who can stand when he appears? For he is like a refiner's furnace and like fullers' soap. (Malachi 3:1–2)

Fuller's soap is a strong and somewhat caustic soap used to bleach clothing and clean wool.

As Jesus's ministry was winding down, and he was on his way to Jerusalem for the last time, his disciples were still having difficulty understanding his words completely and seeing the big picture. They were confused about what he meant when he said he must suffer and die and go away. In several instances, he had spoken of judging others, judging unfairly, and a judgment to come in which he would be the magistrate.

> And he [God] has given him [Jesus] authority to execute judgment, because he is the Son of Man. (John 5:27)

But he had also told them something that sounded like a contradiction. He said,

> If anyone hears my words and does not keep them, I do not judge him; for I did not come

> to judge the world but to save the world. (John
> 12:47)

It is not. He stated his mission clearly. He did not come into the world at that time to judge and separate people into those heaven or hell bound. He came to provide a way to eternal life for us. Now after his resurrection and ascension, he will be the final arbiter and will judge the world on that last day.

Since Christ has promised to return, let's consider several questions about that event. When will it occur? How will we recognize it when it happens? What are we to be doing in the meantime? The first one is easy to answer. Sometime! People have been trying to determine when Christ will return since his ascension. The early Christians appeared to have believed that it would be almost immediate, certainly within their lifetimes. But Jesus never promised that. Over the centuries, pundits and charlatans have looked for clues in various books of the Bible without success. They have watched the rise and fall of governments and dictators, observed natural events such as volcanoes and earthquakes, tracked the planets and other heavenly bodies, and perhaps as far as I know even read tea leaves. There have been many calculations that have failed thus necessitating recalculations that have also failed. If someone with great fanfare and seriousness predicts a certain date and time, you can be sure of one thing; it may occur a minute before or a minute after but not at the predicted time. Christ made that point very clear when he told his disciples,

> But concerning that day and hour no one
> knows, not even the angels of heaven, nor the
> Son, but the Father only. (Matthew 24:36)

Jesus made a definite statement. He did not go about his ministry dropping clues about when he would return. That also seems to eliminate the ever-popular idea that there are tidbits scattered throughout the Scriptures that, if we are smart enough, can be put together to reveal the date. Speculation is an idle and fruitless activity. The lesson here is: It will happen in God's time.

Probably, there has been as much or more written about how Christ will return and how we will be able to recognize the event than there has been about when it will occur. Some seem to believe that he will return rather quietly to lead an earthly kingdom for a period of time before the final judgment. Others think that he will return in the form of a common human and that we will have to learn to recognize him; after all, there have been a number who have claimed to be the reincarnated Christ. But Jesus has also made plain how the second coming will occur and be recognized. He will not sneak back to earth pussyfooting around to pick up a few latecomers or fight a battle with Satan that has already been won. No, everyone will know.

> Then will appear in heaven the sign of the
> Son of Man, and then all the tribes of the earth
> will mourn, and they will see the Son of Man
> coming on the clouds of heaven with power and
> great glory. And he will send out his angels with
> a loud trumpet call, and they will gather his elect
> from the four winds, from one end of the heaven
> to the other. (Matthew 24:30–31)

Wow! How can we miss it? And if that isn't enough there's more.

> For as the lightning flashes and lights up the
> sky from one side to the other, so will the Son of
> Man be in his day. (Luke 17:24)

Will we know? Will everyone know? I think the answer is yes.

With all the clouds and lightning and thunder, are we to dread the last day when Christ sits in righteous judgment? A number of passages speak of the meeting out of punishment and the repayment of each for what has been done such as Matthew 16:27 and 2 Thessalonians 1:6–10. On the contrary, the Lord has given us assuring words.

> Now when these things begin to take place,
> straighten up and raise your heads, because your
> redemption is drawing near. (Luke 21:28)

He also had words of comfort for his disciples before he was arrested and crucified.

> Let not your hearts be troubled. Believe in
> God; believe also in me. In my Father's house are
> many rooms. If it were not so, would I have told
> you that I go to prepare a place for you? And if I
> go and prepare a place for you, I will come again
> and will take you to myself that where I am you
> may be also. (John 14:1–3)

I am sure that if I'm still alive when Jesus returns, it will be a mind-boggling, knee-buckling event, an event filled with awe and wonder even for believers of the Gospel. However, believers, though they might tremble at his return because it will be awe-inspiring, can stand confidently as brothers and sisters of Jesus.

Jesus is coming soon? How soon is soon? In the time frame of human experiences, Jesus has been gone for a very long time. After all, it's been nearly two thousand years since his resurrection and ascension. People who scoffed or discounted the Lord's return were present even during the time of the early church fathers. It is no different today. Unbelievers ridicule this promise and Christians who hold to it. They say, "Where is this Christ? You are backing a dead horse. We have seen all the signs many times. Natural events, turmoil among nations, economic crashes, innumerable wars, and still no Christ. Be logical, use your head, and recognize it for what it is—a myth and a hoax." So what are believers to do? First, let's address this issue. Both the Old and New Testaments speak to this issue of God's slowness. We humans are an awfully impatient bunch. We want answers to our questions and our prayers, and we want them as soon as possible and most of all to be the answers we want to hear. God has provided some clarification for us, but we may have overlooked it. In the Psalms, King David wrote,

> But you, O Lord, are a God merciful and
> gracious, slow to anger and abounding in stead-
> fast love and faithfulness. (Psalm 86:15)

In the New Testament, the apostle Peter made an even more cogent statement,

> The Lord is not slow to fulfill his prom-
> ise as some count slowness, but is patient toward
> you, not wishing that any should perish, but that
> all should reach repentance. (2 Peter 3:9)

The lesson here: Hold your horses and wait for the Lord.

Now back to the question of what we should be doing as we wait for the Lord's return. First, we must acknowledge our sins and repent. Jesus made that abundantly clear. Once when he was teaching a crowd, he was questioned about an incident in which a number of people were tragically killed and whether they were being punished for a particular sin. Jesus responded that it was not punishment for any specific transgression, but that everyone needed to repent.

> No, I tell you; but unless you repent, you
> will all likewise perish. (Luke 13:5)

That is difficult for us to accept since we do not like to consider ourselves as sinners. In addition, many discount sin, heaven, and hell as archaic and obsolete concepts. William Faulkner made an interesting comment about this in his novel *As I Lay Dying*, "People to whom sin is just a matter of words, to them salvation is just words too." Words are important especially those of God's Word.

Second, we must continue to worship, believe the Gospel, and live as Christians. Our sins have been forgiven, but we must understand and believe that it is through the work of Christ alone and not the result of anything we may do. Since we do not know when Christ will return, we need to be prepared at all times.

> Stay dressed for action and keep your lamps
> burning, and be like men who are waiting for their
> master to come home from the wedding feast, so
> that they may open the door to him at once when
> he comes and knocks. (Luke 12:35–36)

We dare not think that we are too young, too busy, or too sophisticated to bother with faith and Christian life. Many of us seem to believe that there is plenty of time to become serious about our worship life. However, sudden death may derail our long-term plans, or Christ may return to judge us. Do we take a chance and play the odds? There really are no odds in this case. To paraphrase an old Groucho Marx saying, "You bet your eternal life!"

> Therefore you also must be ready, for the
> Son of Man is coming at an hour you do not
> expect. (Matthew 24:44)

For me, all this generates another question. What do we receive for being steadfast in our faith and awarded eternal life? Timothy writes that we will receive a crown of righteousness (2 Timothy 4:8). James says we will receive the crown of life (James 1:12). St. Peter promises a crown of glory (1 Peter 5:4). St. Paul tells us that we will be raised with an imperishable body. But what does that actually mean? And what will we be doing? We will be worshiping the Lord, but the details are more than a little bit sketchy. I am certain that I do not know, and I believe that no one else does either, although again much has been written about heaven. We have been told what the Lord will do for us.

> He [God] will wipe away every tear from their
> eyes, and death shall be no more, neither shall there
> be mourning, nor crying, nor pain anymore, for the
> former things have passed away. (Revelation 21:4)

If this sounds familiar it should. It is a direct reference to and fulfillment of Isaiah 25:8–9 cited in the Promises of the Messiah section. Here is another wonderful promise. The apostle John was given a glimpse of heaven and he passed it along to us.

> After this I looked, and behold, a great multitude that no one could number, from every nation, from all tribes and peoples and languages, standing before the throne and before the Lamb, clothed in white robes, with palm branches in their hands, and crying out with a loud voice, "Salvation belongs to our God who sits on the throne, and to the Lamb!" (Revelation 7:9–10)

It is one of the many astounding things that he was privileged to see and pass along to us.

There is one last question that we need to address. Why are we confident that Christ will return and that any of these promises are certain? In these New Testament days, God himself has provided us with two well-witnessed incredible events. First, Christ's resurrection on Easter Sunday.

> The times of ignorance God overlooked, but now he commands all people everywhere to repent, because he has fixed a day on which he will judge the world in righteousness by a man whom he has appointed; and of this is given assurance to all by raising him from the dead. (Acts 17:30–31)

Second, the coming of the Holy Spirit on Pentecost.

> He who has prepared us for this very thing is God, who has given us the Spirit as a guarantee. (2 Corinthians 5:5)

With the resurrection, God put his stamp of approval on Jesus's work and thereby assuring that we will share in a resurrection like his on the last day. God has also given us the Holy Spirit to work faith in human hearts and to sustain us as we go through life.

Questions for Thought and Discussion

1. Why do you think that neither God nor Jesus informed us of the time of his return to judge the world?
2. It's been a long time since Christ's ascension. Provide some reasons for your belief that he will return.
3. How do you imagine judgment day? How do you think you will feel?

Epilogue

Such is the confidence that we have through Christ toward God.
—2 Corinthians 3:4

If we seriously consider the totality of God's promises, it is impossible not to be amazed and deeply thankful. His remarkable promises to the people of the Old Testament provided them with innumerable blessings and kept them looking forward to the hope of a Messiah or savior to come. We as New Testament children of God have an even better promise. We can look backward to the cross with understanding and appreciation of the fulfillment of those promises in the person of Jesus the Christ. While the Old Testament believers stood behind the cross, we of the New stand in front of the cross knowing that the sacrifice of Christ is complete and atones for our sins. They are gone, once and for all, forgiven. However, we do have something in common with those ancient believers as we too look forward with a hope of eternal life and the Lord's return.

As I think about and evaluate the promises of our God, I have learned that he has promised many things—victory in battle; a homeland for his chosen people; children for longing couples; blessings of all kinds; and mercy and forgiveness of our past, present, and future sins. He has carried out each of them. He has called us to him in many ways in many passages.

> Come, everyone who thirsts, come to the
> waters; and he who has no money, come, buy and
> eat! Come, buy wine and milk without money
> and without price. (Isaiah 55:1)

Jesus supplies that promised water to quench our spiritual thirst. Speaking to a Samarian woman at a well, he said,

> Everyone who drinks of this water will be thirsty again, but whoever drinks of the water that I will give him will never be thirsty again. The water that I will give him will become in him a spring of water welling up to eternal life. (John 4:13–14)

He promised an everlasting covenant through his son Jesus Christ.

> Incline your ear, and come to me; hear, that your soul may live; and I will make with you an everlasting covenant, my steadfast, sure love for David. (Isaiah 55:3)

Thanks be to God!

He has also promised that his Son would return as a judge on the Great Day of the Lord!

> And then they will see the Son of Man coming in clouds with great power and glory. (Mark 13:26)

We await that event to come with confidence. Meanwhile, with the important and attention focusing word, *behold*, he has assured us that we are in good hands.

> Behold, I have engraved you on the palms of my hands; your walls are continually before me. (Isaiah 49:16)

A Final Question for Thought

Are you certain that you will receive eternal life? Why?

Appendices

Appendix 1
God Speaks to Humans

How God made his promises and commandments known is an interesting topic. Patriarchs, prophets, kings, apostles, and even ordinary people received their messages, promises, and instructions from God in a number of different ways. Some received a message in their dream. The patriarch Jacob dreamed about angels going up and down a stairway to heaven (Genesis 28:10–17). God spoke to King Solomon in a dream when he granted him his famous wisdom (1 Kings 3:5–15). When he learned that his betrothed, Mary, was pregnant, an angel appeared to Joseph in a dream to assure him about the situation (Matthew 1:20–21).

Others were given their marching orders in visions in which they were told where to go, who to see, and what to say. In contrast to dreams, visions seem to have occurred to a person who was awake. The great prophet Isaiah had an awe-inspiring vision of the Lord on his throne with seraphim above in which he was sent to address both the people and the king of Judah (Isaiah 6:1–7). Daniel, an Old Testament hero of faith, was standing near the bank of the Tigris River when he had a troubling vision in which he saw a man of astounding appearance and heard a voice speak to him (Daniel 10:4–6). About three in the afternoon, Cornelius, a Roman centurion, had a vision in which he saw and heard an angel instruct him to bring the apostle Peter to Caesarea (Acts 10:1–8). Visions sometimes occurred to someone in the presence of others who did not see the manifestation but felt some effects during the event. Such was the case with Daniel's vision and when Paul was converted on the road to Damascus (Acts 9:7).

Often the appearance of angel messengers overwhelmed the humans involved and cause great fear and trepidation. That was Cornelius's reaction to the incident mentioned above. However, at other times, they appeared in human form. Such was the case when three men, one of whom was the preincarnate Christ, on their way to deal with Sodom and Gomorrah visited Abraham to bring him the promise that his wife Sarah would have a child (Genesis 18:1–3). In another instance, Jacob wrestled all night with a man who also seemed to have been the Lord (Genesis 32:22–29). At other times, it is simply stated, "That the word of the Lord came" to the prophets such as Hosea and Joel. Exactly how that happened and what occurred is a matter of conjecture.

Perhaps the most astounding relationship was that of God with Moses. Certainly, there was something special about that relationship as God himself revealed.

> And he said, "Hear my words; if there is a prophet among you, I the Lord make myself known to him in a vision; I speak with him in a dream. Not so with my servant Moses. He is faithful in all my house. With him I speak mouth to mouth, clearly and not in riddles, and he beholds the form of the Lord." (Numbers 12:6–8)

This is not an exhaustive collection of God's interaction with humans but rather provides examples of those miraculous events.

Appendix 2
The Patriarchs: Founders of the Israelite Tribes

The term *patriarchs* generally means founder or father of a tribe or family line. In the Bible, it refers to a group of men who lived before the time of Moses. The principal patriarchs were Abraham who is revered by the Jews and considered the father of the Jewish nation, his son Isaac, and his grandson Jacob, later renamed Israel. As the ancestors of the later tribes of the Israel nation, Jacob's sons and two of his grandsons can be considered patriarchs as well. Although not as common, the men living between Adam and Abraham, for example, Noah, are sometimes included as patriarchs.

For me, there was a bit of confusion about the number of tribes and how they received their names. Jacob had twelve sons, Ruben, Simeon, Levi, Judah, Zebulon, Issachar, Dan, Gad, Asher, Naphtali, Benjamin, and Joseph. The sons and their mothers are listed in Genesis 35:23–26. Sometimes those sons are said to be the ancestors of the twelve tribes of Israel. However, that is not quite the case. Joseph did not directly establish a tribe. Instead, his two sons Ephraim and Manasseh were adopted and blessed by their grandfather, Jacob, before he died and became ancestors of the tribes known by their names. When the Israelites entered Canaan and received their inheritance as allotted through Joshua, the sons of Levi were not allotted a specific area but rather given cities scattered throughout the nation. They had been blessed for their role in ending the covenant-breaking worship of the golden calf during the Exodus (Exodus 32:29). Therefore, there were then twelve tribal areas or administrative divisions of the land.

Appendix 3
The Levites

The Levites were one of the tribes of Israel. They were the descendants of Levi, one of the twelve sons of Jacob. Members of the tribe held a special place in the nation since the time of Moses and the Exodus. At that time when the Israelites became impatient waiting for Moses to return from speaking with the Lord on Mount Sinai, they broke the covenant by making and worshiping a golden calf idol. The tribe was the only one to rally to Moses's call for those on the Lord's side to come forward and put an end to the situation. As a result, they were blessed and set aside to perform special worship duties for God. The story of the Golden calf and the Levites' response is told in the thirty-second chapter of Exodus. It is another sad example of how we humans are impatient, do not rely on the Lord, and take matters into our own hands.

Levites who were direct descendants of Moses's brother, Aaron, formed the priesthood and were responsible for offering sacrifices for the sins of the people. Those Levites not directly descended from Aaron were given the duty and honor to serve as assistants to the priests and carry out many other tasks supporting worship such as playing musical instruments and singing. The responsibilities and duties are described in the book of Numbers. Their consecration to the Lord is given in the eighth chapter of that book. They first assisted the priests to maintain and move the tabernacle or tent that served as the worship center until the temple was built in Jerusalem by Solomon.

When the Israelites crossed the Jordan River and the land was allotted among the tribes, the Levites were not given a specific area of Canaan as their territory. Instead, as described in the twenty-first chapter of Joshua, they were allotted forty-eight cities with their surrounding pasturelands scattered throughout the nation. A Levite began his duties approximately at age twenty-five and retired at fifty. The job of worship assistant was not a full-time occupation. Instead, they served on a set rotating schedule and most of the time lived in their cities and had other occupations.

Appendix 4
Pentecost

The Christian church observes Pentecost on the seventh Sunday after Easter. Perhaps today, the festival does not receive as much attention as it deserves. After all, it commemorates the amazing out-pouring of the Holy Spirit on the apostles after the Lord's ascension into heaven. Jesus had promised to send a helper to his disciples, and this dramatic event records the fulfillment of that promise.

Pentecost celebrates the special gifts received by the apostles that strengthen and prepare them for the difficult work they were to undertake. The helper arrived with the sound of a great wind and tongues of fire that touched each of the men and enabled them to speak languages they had not known. Peter's powerful sermon and witness that day marked the change of the apostles and other disciples from frightened men into bold champions of the faith. On that day, some three thousand people received the Gospel and were baptized (Acts 2:1–41). The event is sometimes considered to mark the beginning of the Christian church.

The festival actually was an Old Testament celebration held seven weeks and one day after the first day of the Passover. It was a celebration of thanks for the early harvest, and because of its timing, it was known as the Festival of Weeks. It was first mentioned in Exodus as one of the conditions of the covenant God initiated with the Israelites through Moses.

> You shall observe the Feast of Weeks, the firstfruits of wheat harvest and the Feast of Ingathering at the years end. (Exodus 34:22)

It was one of the *if/then* conditions God attached to his promise to drive out the people living in Canaan. His command was to celebrate the festivals in recognition of and thankfulness for God's gifts, and all would go well for the Israelites. It is mentioned as a thanksgiving festival for the harvest in Leviticus 23:15, Numbers 28:26, and Deuteronomy 16:9–10. Sometime later, it became somewhat of a remembrance of the law for the people. That seems to be part of the meaning when it is mentioned in Deuteronomy 16:16 and 2 Chronicles 8:12–13. It is one of the things that links the New Testament church with the Scriptures and festivals of the Old Testament.

About the Author

Dr. Ron Stieglitz grew up on a dairy farm in northeastern Wisconsin. He earned a BS from the University of Wisconsin-Milwaukee and advanced degrees in geology from the University of Illinois. He served a tour in Vietnam with the US Army, worked for the Ohio Geological Survey, and conducted research and taught geology and environment science courses for thirty years at the University of Wisconsin-Green Bay. He has held leadership roles in Lutheran congregations in several states. He loved playing baseball and softball until long after it was time to quit. He now patiently follows the Milwaukee Brewers. A professor emeritus, he lives in Green Bay, Wisconsin, with his wife, Bev. They have four grown children, twelve grandchildren, and two great-grandchildren.